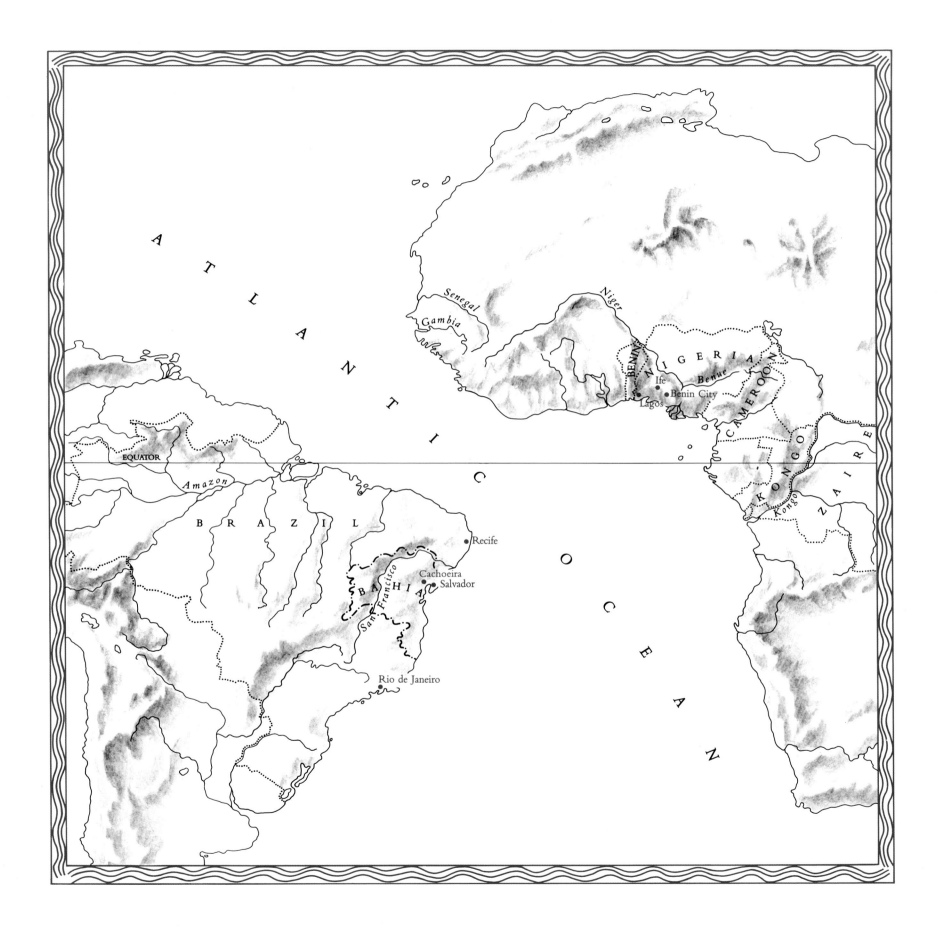

A T L A N T I C

Senegal

Gambia

Niger

BENIN

N I G E R I A

Ife
● ●Benin City
Benue
Lagos

C A M E R O O N

EQUATOR

Amazon

KONGO

Kongo

Z A I R E

B R A Z I L

●Recife

O

Cachoeira
B A H I A ●●Salvador
San Francisco

C

●Rio de Janeiro

E

A

N

ESSAYS BY
ROBERT FARRIS THOMPSON
JOSEPH NEVADOMSKY
NORMA ROSEN
ZECA LIGIÈRO

Foreword by David Byrne

University of New Mexico Press   *Albuquerque*

DIVINE INSPIRATION

From Benin to Bahia

Phyllis Galembo

Library of Congress Cataloging-in-Publication Data

Divine Inspiration: From Benin to Bahia / [photographs by] Phyllis Galembo;
essays by Norma Rosen . . . [et al.]; foreword by David Byrne.

p.   cm.

Includes bibliographical references.

ISBN 0-8263-1377-9 (cloth).   ISBN 0-8263-1378-7 (paper)

1. Benin City (Nigeria) — Religious life and customs.
2. Bahia (Brazil: State) — Religious life and customs.
3. Religious articles — Nigeria — Benin City — Pictorial works.
4. Religious articles — Brazil — Bahia (State) — Pictorial works.
5. Candomblé — Pictorial works.
I. Galembo, Phyllis. II. Rosen, Norma.

BL2480.D3D58   1993

299'.6 — dc20   92-2340

                                          CIP

Printed in Hong Kong

Contents

Foreword

Phyllis Galembo's photographs are frozen waterfalls, forces of nature waiting to be activated. She has taken the nineteenth-century formal portrait and re-energized it, infusing it with the Afro-American spirit. They are a dance for the eyes.

The Afro-Atlantic religions are theater of the most profound sort, where the gods themselves are there in front of us. And in these photos, here they are. The sitter as god! The subject as the embodiment of the deep forces of nature and the cosmos. Well, almost. The people in Galembo's portraits are not actually in the trance possession state, which is normally the only time they would array themselves in the gods' finery. Here they present themselves as potential vehicles, symbolically arrayed in the finery of the god that rules and protects their head. The sitter as living altar! A dancing metaphor.

The altar, meanwhile, is sacred sculpture. It is "visual jazz," constantly reworked and reactivated. It is "played," like a musical instrument. The improvisational aesthetic is, we see, not confined to music. Even the "costumes" are also art as process; they are never "finished" or static. Both they and the altars crumble, melt, rot, and decay like a living being . . . and are constantly being renewed. The "artworks" must be fed. They gain strength through use.

The altar is a mental and spiritual landscape. The terrain of the soul. An energy field. A language beyond conscious understanding. A road map through sacred territory; a set of vertices in spiritual space that help us navigate and get our bearings; a mnemonic device to help us remember what we've always known.

Here we see one aspect of the Afro-Atlantic tradition as it should be seen: in context (at least partially). Traditionally, we see costumes and religious sculpture removed from their surroundings, spotlit in a white room: the contemporary Western idea of giving an object a sacred aura. Granted, the objects are striking and they maintain a portion of their power, but it's like looking at one of Elvis's suits and trying to deduce what made him mean so much to so many people.

The Afro-Atlantic tradition is oral, visual, and musical, rather than written. It won't stay still, it's constantly in motion. It is continually revised and re-created as it passes down from generation to generation. The contemporary generation accepts and incorporates whatever it fancies from the twentieth-century image and icon bank. So, naturally, some of what might be considered traditional techniques are abandoned and new ones are invented. Debates over "correctness" abound, but they're futile. Anything can be made sacred.

This is an aesthetic that, in some meaningful ways, has more in common with today's television generation than with traditional Western art values. The present Western generation, raised on African-inspired pop music, is already unwittingly in sympathy with the ecstatic spirituality manifested here. We've already absorbed some of this through the "subtext" latent in our own popular culture. The same culture which gave us the t.v., the Bomb, rock, funk, and disco has led us to reconsider our past and reevaluate our own foundations. I'm sure it was unintentional. Western culture imports the seeds of its own destruction. A joyful, ecstatic destruction. The very culture that could tear us apart might, inadvertently, bring us together. Galembo's images and the culture they manifest couldn't have come at a better time.

— David Byrne
Los Angeles
January 1992

A Note on the Typography

Two Nigerian languages are used extensively throughout the text of this book: Èdó and Yorùbá. (There are also a few words of Ìgbò and other Benue-Kwa languages.) Starting in the 1860s, the standard writing systems of Nigerian languages have been based on the Roman alphabet, modified by the addition of diacritic marks below and above the letter. A *subdot* [̣] is used to signal the vowels ẹ ị ọ ụ [ɛ ɪ ɔ ʊ] and the consonant ṣ [ʃ]. Certain accent marks over vowels indicate *tone*: acute [´] for high tone, grave [`] for low tone, and the macron [¯] for downstep or mid tone (depending on the language). (In Yorùbá, mid tone is marked only over *m* and *n*.) Without such diacritics, Roman spellings of words in these languages would be either ambiguous (taken out of context) or else simply meaningless. One would be unable to distinguish the Ògùn River from the divinity Ògún, or to tell a house (*ilé*) from the ground (*ilẹ̀*). This book uses the official Nigerian writing systems in the interest of accuracy as well as out of respect for speakers of these languages, many of whom keenly read books written about them in the West. Indeed, there is no excuse to do otherwise, now that technical limits on printing fonts are being overcome by advances in computer typesetting. Naturally, this newfound ease of printing diacritics has brought increased opportunities to make typographical errors! There would have been many more errors in this text had it not been for the generous help of Professor R. Abíọ́dún and Professor R. N. Agheyisi.

— *Victor Manfredi*

Preface

The reader may rightly ask what there is—apart from the happenstance of a photographer's travels and professional acquaintances—to justify the pairing of Nigeria's Benin City (called Ẹ̀dó) with the Brazilian city of Salvador (commonly called Bahia). The title of this book does not imply that any Brazilian shrines or divinities have a specifically Ẹ̀dó origin, as opposed to some other African source. Rather, there is a more general relationship between the two places. From the works by Verger, Herskovits, and Cabrera among others, we know that the Atlantic slave brought people of diverse African origins to the Western Hemisphere. Major African priesthoods in the Americas trace their origins to such kingdoms as Ilé-Ifẹ̀, Ẹ̀dó (Benin), Àgbòmé (Dahomey—in the present République du Bénin), and Kongo. Historians have not yet traced the precise relationships among these ancient states.

Still, why these two places in particular? Beyond the fact that they are both centers of ritual activity, there is one feature which led me as a visual artist to juxtapose Ẹ̀dó and Brazilian shrine photos. This feature is their shared system of religious beliefs and ritual practice, as expressed in images, performances, and songs. Any visitor can see that Bahia and Benin City share a special interest in the divinity of the ocean, known respectively as Iemanjá/Ólókūn. Other shared deities even have the same name: Ogum/Ògún the god of war and iron; Xangô/Èsàngó, the god of thunder and lightning, and so on. In Brazil one refers to axé, the ritual power to make things happen; in Benin City this power is called isẹ́ (= Yorùbá àṣẹ). The idea of divinity is named orixá in Brazil, òsà in Benin (= Yorùbá òrìṣà).

Coming from the bustling asphalt terrain of New York, I responded directly to the urban face of the orixá tradition in Benin City and Brazil. The art of these shrines resonated strongly with a series of photographs which I had developed during the 1970s when I photographed ritual aspects of non-Western theatrical costumes and tableau settings. Personally, I accept the orixá priestesses and priests in their role as diviners who use shrine symbols to guide people through complex, predestined life-patterns. Through photographs, I have tried to approach this process respectfully, gazing through the shrine doors (only as far as non-initiates are allowed), not as a touristic voyeur but as a sympathetic, participant-documenter.

My first access to Èdó shrines was arranged by Norma Rosen, who invited me to Benin City in 1985 to document her research on the design and use of traditional altars and regalia. As a full initiate in the religion of Ólókūn, Ms. Rosen helped me gain access to many people and places. I am extremely grateful to her for this inside exposure to the culture. I would also like to thank her for her essay and drawings and for contributing songs and stories which give the photographs an Èdó voice.

In interpreting these shrine images, I obtained historical and cultural context from two academic friends: Joseph Nevadomsky then of the University of Benin, Benin City, and Robert Farris Thompson of Yale University. I thank Zeca Ligièro, Brazilian playwright, for his contribution on candomblé, and Gisèle Cossard for offering me the chance to consult her unpublished 1970 Sorbonne thesis on ceremonies in a Bahian terreiro. I owe special thanks to Brian Head of the University of Albany, State University of New York, Albany, for translating Zeca Ligièro's essay and for other help throughout the project.

Photographic research in Nigeria and Brazil was sponsored by my family, the Visual Artists Program of New York State Council on the Arts, the Center for Photography at Woodstock, the Faculty Research Awards Program and the Targeted Research Awards Program at the University of Albany, State University of New York, the Fulbright Commission of Brazil, the United States Information Service, Brazil, United University Professions, and a Pan Am Travel award. Polaroid Corporation donated film for instant portrait work, which proved indispensable to the project.

I was ably assisted in Nigeria by Pius Guobadia, Agbonifo Ovenseri, and Sam Igunwe, and in Brazil by Lori Nelson, Carlos Pereira, Andrea Novaes Ferraz, and Luis Llagno dos Santos. The book could not have been completed without the help of Marijo Dougherty, Daniel

Dawson, Pierre Verger, Charles Hagen, Peter Kloehn, Zheng Hu, Joanne Lue, Karen Kramer, Miriam Jacobs, Anne Turyn, Lisa Aronson, John Pfahl, John Dwyer, Martin Adler, Joan Nwuga, Irene Kubeyinje, Ezenuegbe, Igiohen Uyikpen, Clodomir Menezes, Mãe de Santo Olga de Alaketo, Patricia Huntington, Robert Pfehlan, Naomi Katz, Guttenberg, Nelson Cequeira, Maria Brandão, June Ellen, René Ribeiro, Lilian Goes, David Fleisher, Barbara Hitchcock of Polaroid, Mary Virginia Swanson of Swanstock, Peter Andersen, Mãe Mirinha de Portão, Deoscoredes e Juana dos Santos, the Nigerian Consulate, New York, Chief Priest Anthony Ogiemwanye, and Chief Nosa Isekhurhe of Benin. Thanks also to Willis Hartshorn, Marie Spiller, and Lisa Dirkes of the International Center for Photography, Dana Asbury and Milenda Nan Ok Lee of the University of New Mexico Press, and Charles Ellertson at Tseng Information Systems. Final coordination and editing of the text was done with substantial assistance from Ùyínmwẹ̀n Victor Manfredi.

I dedicate this book to my parents, Norman and Rhoda Galembo, and to the priestesses and priests in Nigeria and Brazil who kindly invited me into their shrines.

—Phyllis Galembo
New York City

Divine Inspiration

Not Cuba—which Gauguin never saw,
Picasso never saw—
where blacks clothed in yellow and cherry red
haunt, between two lights,
a boulevard beside the sea.

—Alfonso Reyes, "Gulf of Mexico" (1934)

Divine Countenance

Art and Altars of the Black Atlantic World

ROBERT FARRIS THOMPSON

Mediation, meditation, and conviction—these qualities succinctly define the Afro-Atlantic altar in action. In the outpourings of pottery, for assuagement of unseen winds and powers, in the richness of ideographically emblazoned cloths, murals, and icons, proclaiming the moral grandeur of the spirits, Afro-Atlantic altars announce an important tradition of visual discourse and moral action.

In 1968, Alejo Carpentier published a detailed commentary on an Afro-Cuban altar near Havana. Spiritually aligned with Alfonso Reyes's 1934 declaration of black Cuba's artistic independence from European vogue, Carpentier elaborated the elements of this black altar, tended by a priestess of the Yorùbá-Cuban religion, and showed how the images in it coalesced to create a visual language which, he implied, was stronger than the confected surprise of Western Surrealism.

Carpentier's article set the stage for the serious study of Afro-Atlantic altars as instruments of creative philosophic expression. Today, Africanist literature has begun to move in an analogous direction, as witness George Preston's examination of African sacred objects in their proper reverential series, or Bernard de Grunne's recent observation that "monumental statuary among the Bamana in Mali were made to be seen in groups in the same shrine with mother and child figures, hunters, and equestrian figures. The birth, flourishing, and multiplication of shrines form a key to any art historical analysis for many groups in Africa"

I

(1990: 42). This holds true for all groups in sub-Saharan Africa, from the hunters-and-gatherers of the Ituri and the Kalahari to the city-dwelling Yorùbá and Bakongo.

Altar history, by definition, is concerned with reinstating a sense of the philosophic richness of these ritual sites. The tradition today reaches a level where Yorùbá descendants in Cuba and New York compare notes with Yorùbá-speakers of Nigeria, regaining lost nuance, achieving unsuspected densities in a process known to the Latinos as *recopilación*.[1] It is in this spirit of *recopilación* that one can undertake—with the help of Phyllis Galembo's photographs—an examination of certain altars of the Nigerian city of Ẹ̀dó ("Benin City") and the Afro-Brazilian cities of Salvador, Recife, and Cachoeira.

This consideration can be preceded by a look at sub-Saharan hunter-and-gatherers' natural altars, the forest, the tree, and the fork between two branches. These sites suggest the forest as an eternal focus of sub-Saharan worship, the ultimate place for acts of gratitude and for the rich expression of reflective life. Concomitantly, signs of the power of the forest, such as raffia, stones, and strangely shaped or twisted roots or branches, reemerge in the urban altars of the Sudan, Nigeria, and especially Kongo. Such images also formed part of a vital if invisible culture which was indelibly etched in the minds of captives taken in the Atlantic slave trade, and therefore inevitably reestablished on New World shores.

Yorùbá shrine traditions have strongly affected the Ẹ̀dó-speaking city of Benin, located southeast of Yorùbáland in Ẹ̀dó State, Nigeria. The same formal heritage shapes the visual imagination of the altar-makers of the "Rome of the Africans," intensely sub-Saharan Bahia, in the northeast of Brazil. There thousands of altars await induction into the pantheon of Afro-Atlantic scholarship. The photographic documentation undertaken by Phyllis Galembo is critical to this changing situation. Like Pierre Verger before her, Galembo fluently links key spiritual centers in Nigeria to the culturally strategic points of their influence within the black Americas. Working essentially within the range of her photographs, this overview compares the altars of two or more of the òrìṣà (Yorùbá deities or spirits) who were here before the world, Èṣù and Ògún, plus a few altars of the deified Yorùbá ancestors, Ṣàngó and Yẹmọja.

The value of the study of altars to the òrìṣà extends far beyond the fields of Africanist and African-Americanist art history, providing a window on tomorrow's North and South America. The *New York Times* reports that the latest census indicates profound changes in the racial composition of the United States (Barringer 1991). The speed at which the nation's racial mix is shifting, as thousands upon thousands of Latin Americans, Caribbean and South American blacks, and others pour into northern cities, exerts a complex fascination. As a result, certain of our urban centers, notably New York, Miami, and Los Angeles, begin to rival ancient Rome or Alexandria as points of multicultural exchange. Here insights and voices from major cultural traditions mix, ideally, in self-exalting ways. As Ben J. Wattenberg, the demographer and author, recently noted, "This is the dawning of the first universal nation [which will] cause some turmoil but on balance [constitutes] an incredibly poetic fact" (Barringer 1991). The spread of an intensely Africanizing spirituality among millions of North American Latinos is part of this process, involving the rise of Yorùbá-Cuban, Kongo-Cuban, and Ejagham-Cuban religious reinstatements in Miami and New York. These changes fuel and define the present study.

Carpentier on a Yorùbá-Cuban (Lucumí) Altar

In 1949 Alejo Carpentier transmuted earlier ethnomusicological research on the European, African, and Haitian sources of Cuban popular music into one of the literary classics of the hemisphere, *Kingdom of This World.* The degree and depth of his cultural preparation were, therefore, superb for the task he undertook in 1968 of documenting the importance of the Afro-Atlantic altar.[2] Specifically referring to the lucumí manner of shaping and suggesting transcendence, he intimated that Afro-Cuban altar structures actually could surpass, in their own way, the insights and contributions of the Surrealist revolution. He dared to hint that, compared to the lucumí way of centering objects within spiritual concepts and ideas, Surrealism seemed studied, even inconsequential.

Afro-Atlantic altars glean their "surrealism" from the imagination and faith of the people. The vision stems not from the musings of a handful of privileged white Parisians but from a visual collective composed of women as well as men, unafraid to make daring philosophic points, with altars as places where one enacts conviction. Here objects become co-presences of God and His intermediaries, the oricha (òrìṣà). Carpentier leads us in:

In one corner of a vast room was a fountain full of water from the sea. [Live] fish, collected from the harbor of Havana, swam in this water. The bottom was carpeted with seashells, pieces of glass polished by the sea, starfish, fanshells, different col-ored stones, whatever the sea casts up upon its shores.

In homage to Santa Barbara [Changó, the thunder lord], a warboat floated on the surface: the *Southampton*. Next to the toy destroyer bobbed a barque, of large dimensions, manned by a crew of the "Three Juans" [three men in a boat, lost in a storm, praying to Iemanjá/The Virgin of Regla for salvation]. And from the bounded sea in miniature emerged Solomonic columns, garnished with vine leaf, holding up [a structure in] two stories. On the [first story] surges forward the *Virgen de Cobre*, in a white gown; on the second story appeared a superb *Virgen de Regla*, whose embroidered mantle rested on a globe of the world adorned with anchors and stars. The altar, in its totality, measured two and a half meters high. And there were escorts of fat-cheeked angels, blowing trumpets from the sea. The wall behind the altar was painted with clouds sited on a clear-blue sky. Above, as a finishing-touch…, a sailboat navigates the azure reaches of the skies, a dove of white porcelain suspended from its keel (Carpentier 1968: 222–23).

Carpentier was actually documenting two kinds of altar, one found in nature, the other shaped by the hands of the devotees. Water from the sea is the natural altar of one of the deities honored here, Iemanjá (Yẹmọja), who is also an "oceanic" presence caught in a sacred diorama, extending to infinity her powers of increase and moral intimidation. Out of the brine, like a citation from the High Altar of St. Peter's, Solomonic columns rise. These architectural features praise, in European terms, the majesty and the power of the oricha of the Yorùbá.

In addition, trumpet-playing angels — elements from what the Black Yorùbá of Cuba call èrè òibó, or white man's imagery — are used to suggest the followers of these ancient queens, Iemanjá, goddess of the Atlantic, and Ochun (Ọ̀ṣun), goddess of love and streams. The choice of a white porcelain object as an element is culturally significant. The Yorùbá associate crockery with the white of seashells and the kaolin found at the bottom of the streams, and as a result, white plates, porcelain tureens, whole or in decorative fragments, have been integral elements in the making of altars to important women since time immemorial.

Finally, the altar-maker causes the blue of heaven to blur into the azure expanse of the sea.

A ship crosses these deliberately confused boundaries, carrying a double cargo of the spirit: not only the dove of the Holy Spirit, in Roman Catholic terms, but also the bird of mind and herbalism—the ancient Yorùbá image of medicine which guards all shrines from evil and disease. The metaphorical richness of this altar, a machine for endless prayer and assuagement, is diminished if it is limited to a single interpretation. The vision and imagination of an entire artistic life, the life of the maker of the altar and probably that of her family as well, are at issue here. Her beliefs and those of her family are mirrored in the *dramatis personae* she chooses to honor. Should she need an intimidating man to help her, she summons, through complex punning, Xangô (Ṣàngó), the lord of thunder, with his moral fire and lightning; these powers are vested implicitly in the military fire and smoke of the miniature gunboat. When she seeks to ensure continuity for her family, that her children and her followers may have children, she calls on Iemanjá by aiming her prayer at the richness of the sea. This she suggests by adding to the altar treasures from beneath the water—shells, glass, and other objects. These are presented to the viewer as if in a womb made of water, filled with miniature icons of the mother of the seas, as if heaven and earth themselves had come to term, and were about to give birth.

Galembo's photograph of an altar to Oxum/Iemanjá at Cachoeira, near Salvador, in the northeast of Brazil (Fig. 1) documents a faraway shrine to the same deity honored by Caridad in Havana. Comparison of the black Brazilian altar, prepared and tended by Iyalorixá Baratinha of Ile Kayo Alaketu Axe Oxum, with the one described by Carpentier reveals two shrines operating under the same deep-rooted cultural assumptions and instincts.[3] Both demonstrate the way in which stylistic trends and associative values of the Yorùbá altar-makers of Nigeria live beyond the seas. Thus consider a third altar to the same goddess, this one built and documented in the very city of Yẹmọja (as she is known in Africa), Ibàdàn.[4] The visual traditions combined in the Ibàdàn altar to Yẹmọja suggest the origins of the two New World shrines.

But first compare Galembo's photograph to Carpentier's description. Note the same painted fusion of the domains of the land and sky. In Brazil, Iemanjá frequently blends with the Western image of the mermaid, her naked breasts, fishtail, and long tresses recoding plenitude and endless flowing water. She is identified in Brazil as a sovereign of her element by a crown emblazoned with a star. What the novelist Djuna Barnes called the "obstetric line," the

Figure 1. Iyalorixá Baratinha, Oxum/Iemanjá shrine.

strong curve which traces the belly of a woman come to term, is not unlike the arc of the altar pool filled with water from the bay. In Galembo's image, this in turn is answered by the bell-like hoopskirt of the high priestess, Baratinha, ringing an àájà bell of Nigerian Yorùbá style to gain the attention of her goddess. With deft visual touches Baratinha reclaims the territory of Iemanjá, her powers of feminine beauty and fecundity. A candle provides a western light for the entrance of the deity, while perfumes deepen her attractive femininity. Ibéjì figurines, twin statuettes from Nigeria, emphasize both Iemanjá's African origins and her procreative powers. As in Carpentier's altar in Havana, a miniature boat provides an homologous link to her element. Images of mermaids repeatedly restate her powers to combine the secrets of the sea and the powers of important women. A leviathan of a fish, swimming through the sky, further suggests this mystic world, where oceanic powers elude their common placements.

Meanwhile Iemanjá, in her portrait as a mermaid on the wall, acknowledges with her right hand a stone beside the water, a classical Yorùbá emblem of immortal presence. To traditionally minded Yorùbá, stones in water are spirits in the sea, a connection which may well be captured in miniature by the tureen elevated in the corner of this shrine. The tureen is accompanied by a sailing ship, and adorned with yet another mermaid image. If this vessel contains actual stones of the goddess, immersed in briny sea water, the three rhyming curves—skirt, pool, tureen—contain within their circled emphases the hidden script of Iemanjá. Written in stones and brine, this is a script of undying ecstasy, of the giving of children from the fluids of the womb, and of the mother's protection of her children, as unyielding as stones in water.

Again, compare the Carpentier and Galembo shrines, this time to a shrine for Yẹmọja in Ibàdàn photographed by Pierre Verger and described by the late Àràbà of Lagos. Many of the same elements can be found in Verger's famous photograph (1954: Plate 166). Here, though, painted backdrops, warships, and mermaids vanish. Instead we view a subtly stated, compact series of images, two of them sealed and augmented in swaths of cloth, all set against a plain wall. The goddess, cloth cascading from her head on either side, is mirrored by a minor female figure, representing a devotee or daughter. This figure, too, is decked with cloth. The women tower over the altar, like two textile-marked triangles. Yẹmọja is surrounded by a carving of a policeman, an image of a woman bearing gifts in a calabash container, two chickens, three Toby figures, and a cat. There is also a calabash, resting in an enamel container, itself bearing a picture of a sailing ship.

The Àràbà decodes this altar in terms of the exegetic oral divination literature of Ifá, grand document of Yorùbá lore and culture.[5] First, he notes, the image of Yẹmọja wears the cascading strip of cloth "because Yẹmọja is possessed of infinite cloths and garments as sign of her mastery over Gẹlẹdẹ" and its comparably cloth-decked images. Yẹmọja, so it is believed in some parts of southern Yorùbáland, "gave birth to Èfè [the night ceremony of Gẹlẹdẹ] and Gẹlẹdẹ [the afternoon performance] and Tètèdé [the first singing mask to arrive at the Èfè night performance]."[6] In other words, two of the altar icons are associated by their textiles with the pageantry and songs of moral admonition associated with Èfè. The flowing cloth helps to enshrine the spirit of Yẹmọja-Gẹlẹdẹ and her daughter, even as cloth is the important indication of numinous presence in the worship of the moral inquisitors called Egúngún in other aspects of Yorùbá traditional worship. (In fact, the Àràbà referred to this cloth as agọ̀, the Egúngún term.)

The porcelain cat, humanized by presenting its front paws in a gesture of giving, refers to the catching of the bush-rat [eku], "which Yẹmọja and her children ate in stews and which was used in the making of a medicinal 'concoction.'" Rooster and hen allude to sacrifice, undertaken "to enhance the eku soup of Yẹmọja for her children." The image of a woman with a calabash container restates the theme of giving, while security is suggested by the standing icon of a policeman or bodyguard. In this atmosphere of respect, entourage, and sacrifice, the ample girth of Yẹmọja reveals her as full-buttocked [ìdí lálá] Yẹmọja-Gẹlẹdẹ, "who gives birth to countless children." "Give richly," the altar suggests (through its cloth, chicken, and bush-rat), "and Yẹmọja will give back children and protection." The gift of children is further recorded by the addition of three Toby figures imported from the world of English vernacular pottery. They are not Europeans, the Àràbà suggests [wọn kì ń ṣe òyìnbó]. They are children of Yẹmọja, whom she lovingly powders in gleaming crimson osùn paste: "They are the children who usually surround her."

A last element, seemingly insignificant, actually harbors the central point of this altar. The metal container, emblazoned with an image of a sailing ship, contains actual river stones, emblematic of Yẹmọjás immortal presence, which are immersed in water, gathered from the River Ògùn, her most proximate domain in the region of Ibàdàn. In some parts of Yorùbáland, it is believed that to drink of a broth steeped in stones will give health and longevity, by analogy to the time-resistant qualities of all stones.[7] Moreover, Yorùbá say not only òyìgíyigì ọta omi, "hard stone from the spring of water, emblem of great strength," but also àwa di òyìgíyigì, "we become stones in water," and a à kú mọ́, "we die no more."[8] And so the altar becomes, at the end, inherently ideographic. Yorùbá altar statuary and embellishment are thus profoundly linked to proverbs and moral admonition.

Leaf, Branch, and Tree: Dawn of the Black Altar

For the Mbuti of the Ituri Forest in northeast Zaire, the forest is God. "The forest is the permanent guarantee of man's duration" (Dupré 1970: 152). An altar, where one appropriately renders gratitude and belief; an oceanic, all-encompassing shrine found in nature — this is the forest of Mbuti. Thus, after successful hunting, when the cooking is done, "little pieces of food are laid aside on a leaf [for the forest spirits]" (Dupré 1970: 153). And again, when an important animal is killed, a piece of the heart of the beast (or another organ) is cast into the

for luck and fortune. The altar to earth includes an intriguing, small cruciform motif. This object symbolizes the crossroads of wet and dry seasons, of day and night: "Remove day or night, or dry or wet, and everything falls down." The sign of the cross, in Bini terms, thus voices imperatives of moral continuity. It warns that to transgress the laws of the ancestors and of God is like trying to subtract day from night, or blocking the coming of rain at the end of the season of dust and heat.

Next to the altar to God appears a powerful emblem, the eye of God. Two porcelain plates embedded on the wall flank this all-seeing emblem. These circles of porcelain symbolize "the earth, the representation of the circle of the earth." The plates may also constitute visual loan-translations of the original use of the calabash containers as emblems of the world in Yorùbá symbolic thought. "Here one prays with chalk, here one never slaughters animals. White is purity, red is authority." But on this august dais, of chalk-traced purity, there stands a strong staff ending with a closed-fist motif. This signifies: "tight control, take control of your destiny." Can this decode, as well, the closed-fist Gara figure, from Nigerian antiquity?

Earth is thus the mirror. Through earth all prayers reach the gods. But the altar also instructs. The objects on the dais teach servitors how to capture effectiveness (lick thunderstones), how to recognize and call upon your ancestors (count the ùkhùrhẹ, memorize their former owners), how to visualize imperatives (comprehend the cross), how to effect a certain kind of mystic healing (bring in leaves of èwèrè), how to master destiny (mime the fist on the altar staff). In other words, this Yorùbá-influenced shrine challenges the viewer in a fundamental way. It warns him that he draws his strength as much from what remains to be done, as from that which he now asks. This is the challenge. Face the gods and make sacrifice to them, in exchange for this or that requirement. But, always, they stare back. Nothing is easy. The price of life, of happiness, is paid in later acts, as well as present words and gifts. The gaze of the Èdó altar, coded materially, commands the future while explaining the past. Consequently, Èdó, guarded and instructed by such altars, remains imperturbably itself.

An Altar to Èṣù in Nigeria / to Exu in Brazil

A Yorùbá divination priest explained to me in Lagos why the classic altar to Èṣù-Ẹlẹgbáa in Nigeria became a mound of laterite into which a carved wooden penis, in a state of sexual excitement, was inserted. The element visually recodes the deity's famous praise-poem: *okiri*

Figure 6. Exu, Terreiro Oxá Furu, Salvador, Brazil.

oko ki oko, which means "strongest of all erections, hardest of all hard-ons."[13] In other words, Èṣù is a lover on a heroic scale. Whether you call him Exu or Zé Pilintra in Brazil, he never loses this basic trait. In fact, his way with words and women, his ability to transgress boundaries renders, in an all-too-human way, a metaphor for his powers of communication, as messenger to the gods. The same source says Èṣù became a lateritic mound in order to hide the scarring of his body. According to tradition, Èṣù once stupidly enraged Ṣònpònnó, the lord of pestilence and fever, by poking fun at his lameness. For this arrogance, Ṣònpònnó severely pock-marked the body of Èṣù, forcing him to hide in laterite. Shame, and the wages of excess or arrogance, are thus lessons written in the structure of this altar. In addition, black, the color of shame, remains one of the distinguishing symbols of Èṣù, in frequent association with bright red, another violent, clashing shade. Both colors become trans-Atlantic renderings of his name. One sacrifices, then, before the mound with protruding membrum in order to guard oneself from contingency, from unknown intrusions by unknown persons who might destroy us in their careless pleasures or mindless arrogance.

In Dahomean compounds, west of Yorùbáland, multiple figureated laterite altars have been erected to Legba, the local offshoot of Ẹlẹ́gbáa. They guard the compounds, one to each servitor of the spirit. In Brazil, Dahomean Legba and Yorùbá Èṣù-Ẹlẹ́gbáa come together in creole fusions, with extraordinary results. We see how Brazil deepens and transforms essentials of the Yorùbá Èṣù altar. The lateritic mound is transformed into earthen mounds built up in dishes, each a different avatar of Exu. Many of them bristle with tridents which variously pun on crossroads [orìta], the classic point of transition and provocation over which Exu reigns. But the trident also associates a misreading of Èṣù's moral provocations with Satan, which simultaneously forgets Èṣù's indispensable role as messenger to the gods. Each mound or image of Exu is also different, for he is the very spirit of human individuality, with all the attendant dangers which accompany going out alone to make one's mark in the world. The roseate tone of the shrine walls somewhat mutes Exu's association with red, color of fire and provocation, repeated more classically in the clash of red and black banners on the wall relieved by a swath of white. These are the colors of spiritual command, axe (àṣẹ). The corners of the altar are guarded with wooden figures which apparently refer to Exu in the guise of elders. Various types of Brazilian pottery—quartinhas, a muringa, and bottles for beer, champagne, and palm oil—are visual investments in his favor. Most impressive is a black stone, color-coded in Exu's name, to the right of the central portion of the altar, which looms up moist with sacrifice out of an offertory bowl. In sum, this altar confronts us with concrete images of contingency, multiple problems, symbolically horned, repeatedly assuaged with liquid and with prayer. This altar, smudged with the blood of sacrifice, seeks with its many trickster-images to expose and unfold the myriad ways by which we can be undone by Accident and Shock, the children of Exu.[14] So constituted, it accentuates the need for sacrifice, to transform danger into calm, jealousy into reconciliation. These altars have been honored and anchored by their ornamental enthronement upon the running dais, as well as by the variety of sophisticated refreshments offered in their name. A relentless search for redemption drives this careful orchestration of the forces of provocation and surprise.

We could visit many other altars in the black Atlantic world, for they are literally everywhere—beside a cash register on Thirty-sixth Street in Manhattan; on the beach of Copacabana on New Year's Eve; on a bank of the Ọ̀ṣun River in Nigeria; under a Ceiba tree one block from Revolution Plaza in Havana. All, together, suggest "Afro-Atlantis" as a fabulous emergence, a mind counted in prayer and garlanded in aspirations.

Notes

1. I thank Professor David Brown of Emory University for bringing this important concept in contemporary Latino worship to my attention.

2. For an excellent study of Carpentier's position in world literature, see Gonzalez 1977.

3. I am grateful to Iyalorixa Baratinha for allowing me to study and photograph her altar in the summer of 1988 in Cachoeira.

4. Ògùn State is named after the River Ògùn and not after the divinity Ògún.

5. From a series of interviews conducted at his compound in Èkó (Lagos), January 1983.

6. For details, see Drewal and Drewal 1983.

7. Àràbà Èkó, Lagos, January 1983.

8. Bishop J. Johnson, quoted in Dennett (1906: 255).

9. For the legend of the birth of men and women, set free by a chameleon spirit from the insides of a tree, see Dupre (1970: 159).

10. Àràbà Èkó, Lagos, January 1983. The *oriro* is also called *ooro*.

11. Àràbà Èkó, Lagos, January 1983. I have heard similar testimony from other Ifá priests.

12. Chief Nòsá Ìsèkhùrhè, Ìsèkhùrhè N'Èdó, Benin City, 22 August 1989. All citations relating to this shrine are from Chief Ìsèkhùrhè, to whom I am indebted for the care and fullness of his explanations.

13. Àràbà Èkó, Lagos, January 1983.

14. According to Àràbà Èkó (Lagos, January 1983), Ifá says that Accident and Paralysis are children of Èsù. I have retranslated Paralysis as Shock, in the sense of a traumatic stoppage of the normal flow of the world, testing the pretentious and the self-absorbed.

References

Abíọ́dún, R., H. J. Drewal, and J. Pemberton. *Yorùbá: Nine Centuries of African Art and Thought.* New York: Center for African Art, 1989.

Bahuchet, S. and G. Philippart de Foy. *Pygmées: Peuple de la forêt.* Paris: Denoël, 1991.

Barringer, F. "Census shows profound change in racial makeup of the nation, " *New York Times,* March 11, 1991, p. 1.

Carpentier, A. *El Reino de este mundo, Relato.* Mexico City: Edición y Distribución Iberoamericana de Publicaciones, 1949.

Carpentier, A. "Los altares de la Caridad," *Islas* 10.1 (1968).

Dennett, R. E. *At The Back of The Black Man's Mind.* London: Cass, 1906, 1968.

Drewal, J. H. "Ifẹ̀: Origins of Art and Civilization," In Abíọ́dún *et al.* 1989.

Drewal, J. H., and M. T. Drewal. *Gẹ̀lẹ̀dẹ́: Art and Female Power among the Yorùbá.* Bloomington: Indiana University Press, 1983.

Dupré, W. *Religion In Primitive Cultures.* The Hague: Mouton, 1970.

Fitts, D. (ed.) *Anthology of Contemporary Latin-American Poetry.* Norfolk, Connecticut: New Directions, 1942.

Garlake, P. E. "Excavations at Ọbalárá's land, Ifẹ̀, Nigeria," *West African Journal of Archaeology* 4 (1974): 111–48.

Gonzalez Echevarria, R. *Alejo Carpentier: The Pilgrim at Home.* Ithaca: Cornell University Press, 1977.

Grunne, Bernard de. "The concept of style and its usefulness in the study of African figurative sculpture," In *Afrikanische Skulptur: Die Erfindung der Figura.* Koln: Museum Ludwig, 1990.

Turnbull, C. M. *The Mbuti Pygmies: An Ethnographic Survey.* New York: American Museum of Natural History, 1961.

Verger, P. *Dieux d'Afrique.* Paris: Paul Hartmann, 1954.

For his clear and sympathetic editing, I thank Charles Hagen—in whose presence the last paragraph of my essay was written, New York, July 1991. I also acknowledge the impact on my essay of Babátúndé Lawal's important study,"Ojúbọ: The Art and Meaning of the Yorùbá Altar," presented at the College Art Association Annual Conference, Washington, D.C., in February 1991. Particularly enlightening is the way Lawal shows us that "shrine furniture" may actually encode deep-rooted ideographic allusions to the protocols of proper action before the spirit.

— *Robert Farris Thompson*

Religious Symbolism
in the Benin Kingdom

JOSEPH NEVADOMSKY

At the time of British colonization at the end of the nineteenth century, the Nigerian landscape featured kingdoms and empires of great antiquity. The savanna region was governed by Hausa-Fulani and Kanem-Bornu emirates which—with the power of cavalry and Islam—had expanded beyond the borders of older, non-Islamic kingdoms. To the south, in the equatorial forest among speakers of Kwa and Benue-Congo languages flourished a great variety of religious and political systems.

All southern Nigerian groups—together with their West African neighbors of the forest belt—draw on a common heritage of several thousand years: a fund of similarities in language, ideas, and practices. For example, there is an archaic, numerological divination system known in Yorùbá as Ifá, in Ìgbò as Áfá, and in Ẹ̀dó as Ìhà. Local variants of this system cover all of southern Nigeria. Beyond this shared foundation, processes of mutual influence have spread other cultural and political features across the area. For example, the divinity Èsàngó came to Benin within the past few centuries, from his origin in the Yorùbá-speaking kingdom of Ọ̀yọ́.

Despite these similarities, however, we can contrast two broad social types within Nigerian rain forest civilization. In the southwest, Yorùbá-speaking peoples built urbanized, militarized kingdoms, tied together by symbols of shared descent and religion.[1] In the southeast, Ìgbò, Èfìk-Ìbìbìò and Ìzọ̀n-speaking peoples lived in autonomous villages, linked mainly by trade.[2] The Ẹ̀dó-speaking peoples combined elements of both types.

Claiming historical affiliation with Ilé-Ifè, which is the most sacred Yorùbá monarchy, the Èdó Kingdom (usually called "Benin" in English) surpassed even the Yorùbá city-states in centralization and the ritualization of state politics. Èdó villages, by contrast, resembled small, dispersed settlements such as typify the Ìgbò-speaking area. Massive trade and tribute supported the Èdó palace, which occupied roughly half of the traditional city area, while the villages sustained themselves and paid their taxes mainly from hunting and rain forest horticulture. Spanning these twin poles, Èdó society remains distinctive, even in the mercantile and industrial context of modern Nigeria.

Unlike both the Ìgbò and the Yorùbá, the Èdó (or "Bini") have shallow, nonlandholding patrilineages. The village as a whole allocates farmland. Then and now, however, wealthy individuals may cultivate personal plantations with hired labor. Èdó society also puts an exceptional emphasis on primogeniture: the eldest son takes the main share of his father's property, including heritable titles and privileges. However, the Èdó also resemble the Ìgbò — and differ from the Yorùbá — in emphasizing age-based authority. The male population of a village divides into youths, adults, and elders; traditionally, the junior age grade is assigned to public works, the adults to community defense, and the elders to judicial and ritual tasks. Chiefly titles reflect a combination of patronage (as with the Yorùbá) and personal achievement (as with the Ìgbò). There are two kinds of village chiefs: the nonhereditary òdiónwéré, the oldest male, and the ònógiè, a descendant or client of the Óbá. Then and now, young village men make their way to the capital to seek their fortune, to serve the Óbá (king) and to climb the palace hierarchy.

The growth of the Èdó Kingdom from various chiefdoms can be retraced archaeologically in its vast system of ramparts; these began as village boundaries which gradually merged until today they constitute the longest earthworks in the world. The walls suggest that one village ministate began to incorporate its neighbors sometime in the thirteenth or fourteenth centuries. Oral tradition surrounds the rulers of these communities in heroic legends, giving them the title Ògìsó, "Sky-King." One of these early rulers gained legitimacy by associating himself to the nearby Yorùbá kingdom of Ifè (which the Èdó call Úhè). As retold in Èghárévbá's history, Éwèká, the founder of the present dynasty, was the son of the holy Ifè king. As Éwèká's lineal descendant, every Óbá of Benin rules by "divine right." To this day, the division between the "alien" palace and the "indigenous" town continues to have both ritual and political relevance. For example, during every coronation ceremony, the new Ọ́bá symbolically "buys" the land from the descendents of the first "owners."

The Ẹ̀dó Empire reached its apogee in the sixteenth century, during the Portuguese coastal trade. At the river port of Úghọ̀tọ́n (or "Gwatto"), just within the barrier of coastal mangrove swamp, European merchants obtained chili peppers, ivory tusks, and eventually slaves in exchange for imported cloth, coral beads, cowries, brass rods, and eventually guns. To control this trade required a political structure flexible enough to assimilate smaller states, but strong enough to enforce its will.

Early foreign visitors, impressed by the size of the city, observed that the streets were longer and wider than in most European cities. They describe the palace as the grandest in West Africa, its large compartments linked by pillared colonnades hung with many hundreds of cast brass plaques depicting victories and pageants.

Its court art has made the Ẹ̀dó Kingdom justly famous around the world. The thousands of carved ivories and cast brass figures and plaques—now scattered in the world's treasure houses—were produced by guilds in the monarch's employ. So favorably do these works compare to the great art of Europe's own antiquity that they were once erroneously thought to have been inspired by it. Any outside influence was much closer to home: the early brass heads probably show the influence of Ilé-Ifẹ̀.3 Later works, for example the memorial brass heads, are more ponderous in style, bearing the weight of an empire in its twilight.

Over five centuries, the office of Ọ́bá was transformed from an aggressive military chief into a sacred ruler, hemmed in by elaborate ceremonial and administrative structures. By the nineteenth century, distant revolts and civil conflicts had shattered the empire, depleted its riches, and left the capital in turmoil. The kingdom itself came to an end in 1897, when a British trade delegation blundered into the middle of the Ìguẹ̀ Festival and tried to break the ritual seclusion of Ọ́bá Òvọ́nrràmwẹ̀n. The consequences were predictable. The brash intruders were attacked and killed by an ambitious war chief. A British punitive expedition, sent to avenge the massacre, burned the city and sacked the palace. Òvọ́nrràmwẹ̀n died in exile. Thousands of artworks were shipped to Europe as war booty.

In 1914 the monarchy was cautiously restored, under the colonial policy of Indirect Rule which had been applied in the Northern Protectorate.4 Ẹ́wẹ̄ká II rebuilt some of the palace. His son Ákẹ́nzuà II graced the throne through forty-five years of colonial, civilian, and military rule. Érédiáùwà, the present incumbent, benefits from a growing consensus that traditional leaders must be included in the national governing process. Far from a spectacular anachronism, Èdó kingship continues to represent the main social reality for many people, providing meaning amidst clashing ideologies, and promising security in a politically unstable time. Although the Ọbá's power is now less than in centuries past, the ideas underlying the kingship persist, through myth and ritual, as a general cognitive model. In status second only to the gods, the Ọbá remains a sacred overlord.

Érédiáùwà has rallied his people by revitalizing archaic kingship rituals. Órò and Ódóduò commemorate events of the distant past. During Ìguè, the Ọbá communes with his own ancestors and sacrifices to his "Head," the mystical source of good and bad fortune for himself and for all of the Èdó. Also in the Ìguè, the Ọbá bestows gifts on his loyal chiefs and replays historic conflicts with the land's original rulers. Such rituals of renewal both rid the kingdom of defilement and restore harmony among the living and the ancestors.

Like the beginnings of the kingdom, the origin of the Èdó world is enshrined in songs, proverbs, and ritual performances which resolve religious paradoxes through everyday symbols. The Èdó place themselves at the center of creation: Èdó-óré-ì-sẹ-àgbọ̀n ("Èdó, the Land that Extended to the Visible World"). Primordial time is seen as a vast expanse of water broken only by a single íkhínmwìn tree. On top of this tree lived ọwọ̀nwọ̀n, the double-casque hornbill, a long-beaked bird which figures prominently in the genesis stories and dance masks of many African peoples. Òsànóbùa, having decided to create the world, sent his three children as intermediaries: Òbièmwẹ̀n (his oldest child, a daughter), Ólókūn, and Ògíùwú. As they were about to depart, ọwọ̀nwọ̀n shouted that they should carry a snail shell with them. When they had paddled their boat to the center of the watery waste, Òbièmwẹ̀n turned the shell upside down and out poured an endless stream of sand, which became dry land. After the cautious chameleon tested the firmness of the ground with its dainty feet, Òsànóbùa shared out the earth among his children. To Òbièmwẹ̀n he gave control over childbirth and agriculture; Ólókūn received the power to bestow wealth; and Ògíùwú became the dispenser of death.

In another version of the myth, summarized by Paula Ben-Amos (1980: 45), Òsànóbùa had three sons: Ólókūn, Ògíùwú, and the youngest who became the king of Benin and owner of the land "even up to the land of the Europeans" (Ọbá yàn òtọ̀ sẹ́ èvbò Ébō). Yet another variant recounts how Òsànóbùa created kings to rule the world. Before they descended from heaven, each was allowed take one gift to humankind. Some chose wealth, crafts, or magic, but the Ọ́bá of Benin carried a snail shell full of sand. "He poured the sand on a point which immediately became dry land. The other kings who had been hovering around without dry land to settle upon had to ask the Benin king for land" (Ẹ́wẹ̄ká 1989:10).

These versions—which all resemble creation stories told in Ilé-Ifẹ̀—are important as mythical charters, and for the religious worship they inspire. The central role they give to the Ọ́bá of Benin suggests a dynamic place for kingship in the natural order of things. At the head of this order, Òsànóbùa the Creator is above human concern and has no established priesthood or institutional worship. Òsànóbùa is a transcendant god rather than an immanent deity. Prayers to him are of a general nature, directed toward the sun (or the direction from which it rises), or recited at modest household shrines consisting of a long ìkhínmwìn pole surrounded by lumps of chalk and cowries. These shrines, called Òsàgbáyé ("God occupies the world"), accept only live offerings, typically a white dove. In the city there are three main Òsànóbùa shrines; one is a large building thought to mark the site of the first Catholic church established by the Portuguese, now seat of the Èdó National church, which consciously blends Christian and Èdó beliefs.

Most accounts of creation omit Òbiẹ́mwẹ̀n, the Creator's female child, whose worship has fallen into abeyance. Melzian's 1937 dictionary fails to mention her; so do more recent compilations (Aigbe 1985, Agheyisi 1986). Ben-Amos reports that there was once an Òbiẹ́mwẹ̀n shrine, to which the Ọ́bá appointed a priest. A few active Òbiẹ́mwẹ̀n shrines still exist in the countryside, but she is now most often named as the senior wife of whatever deity happens to be worshipped in a particular community. Èghárévbá, for example, identified her as a wife of the earth: "mother of all human beings and all living things . . . the source and goddess of breeding" (1946: 84). Her title, Ùhé-nẹ́-író, ("Vulva-opening of the wide road") praises her protection of pregnancy and childbirth. In famine and pestilence, too, people appeal to her for help. Associated with both food and fertility, Òbiẹ́mwẹ̀n may have been an Earth Goddess, corresponding to the Ìgbò divinity Àlà or Ànị̀.

Òbiẹ́mwẹ̀n's diminished glory in creation stories may correlate with the expanded importance of Ólókūn, whose rise in the pantheon probably went hand in hand with increasing wealth from the state monopoly over ocean-going trade. Ọ́bá Ẹ́wūárè, who reigned during the arrival of the Portuguese, is said to have gone to the sea to defeat Ólókūn in a wrestling match and take away his coral beads (ìvié). From that time, the Ọ̀bá's state regalia is a massive suit of coral beads, and the wearing of coral demands a strict code of conduct.

Òkún is the word for ocean and Ólókūn means "Owner of ocean." The ocean's beneficial qualities provide a host of symbols of prosperity, happiness, and fertility. In Ẹ̀dó thought, the land of the living is surrounded by the limitless water into which all rivers flow. Human souls must cross through these waters—Ólókūn's realm—to be born or depart on their way to the spirit world after death. The homonym òkún is also the name of a large box, decorated with mirrors and white cloth, used symbolically in mortuary rites to contain the deceased's wealth and status. Both objects represent Ólókūn.

Today Ólókūn is the focus of intense worship. Nearly every household has Ólókūn altars, one for every woman, and perhaps a central one for the household head. Shrine objects include clay waterpots (ùrù) and miniature brass ladders and canoes with paddles that symbolize the worshipper's desire for social mobility. Òrhuè (riverside white chalk or kaolin), with its generic sense of purity and happiness, is ubiquitous. Someone who receives good news is said to have "a stomach full of chalk" (ẹ̀kò nẹ́ ọ̀ òrhuè). Cowrie shells are another object which evokes Ólókūn. The monetary use of cowries—with their deep symbolism of prosperity—lasted well into this century. Cowries also figure in divination, shielding their possessor from harm.

Every four days (the traditional Ẹ̀dó week), a shrine's members gather to invoke Ólókūn, beseech him with requests, and receive his blessings. The central preoccupation of Ólókūn worship is the control of human fertility. When Ólókūn grants children to women, they prosper and rise in social status. A barren woman holds a tenuous position in society, as her marriage is threatened by the lack of children. Those who have no children are anxious to conceive; those who are fertile pray for more. Since the Ẹ̀dó hold the woman responsible for childlessness as well as for a child's sex (important in a strongly patrilineal system), there is little wonder that Ólókūn is heavily patronized by women.

Worshippers also believe that Ólókūn can increase their wealth: Ólókūn ghá khián gbé òvbọ̀khà, ọ ghì yá íghó giè ẹ̀ré ("When Ólókūn went to kill a youth, he gave him money instead"). If one is fortunate, one's Ólókūn shrine may be fittingly enlarged. While the typical shrine consists of chalk lumped around the essential ritual pot, shrines commissioned by the wealthy may fill an entire chamber or room with tableaux depicting Ólókūn, his wives, and courtiers arrayed in a palace beneath the sea, enthroned and dressed in coral and cowrie regalia. Some Ólókūn are known by the name of one of Ólókūn's many wives who is then the central sculpture, for example Ìmẹ̀nẹ̀ the favorite wife, Ákpòwá the faithful servant, Ìgbàghọ̀n the beautiful concubine.

Ólókūn's role resembles that of Màmí Wàtá, who also controls wealth and fertility. A deity popular in the nearby Niger delta, Màmí Wàtá is also worshipped in Benin City. Èghárévbá calls Màmí Wàtá Ólókūn's favorite wife (1946:84). Ólókūn and Màmí Wàtá share the same universe of meaning. Ólókūn is sometimes confused with Màmí Wàtá and described as female. Some symbols are common to both deities, for example mirrors which represent water, trance possession, and vehicles to the other world. Other symbols are particular: kaolin chalk for Ólókūn, perfumed talcum powder for Màmí Wàtá Ólókūn worshippers dance to the percussive music of úkúsẹ̀, a calabash covered with stringed beads; Màmí Wàtá priestesses perform with harmonica and guitar. One of Ólókūn's praise epithets, Ọ̀bá-nẹ̀-àmẹ̀ ("God of the sea") applies more generally to any river deity including Màmí Wàtá and Ólókūn's many wives. A statue said to depict Ọ̀bá-nẹ̀-àmẹ̀ was recently placed in a fountain setting near the palace. The statue is that of woman wearing a coral-beaded crown and other kingship apparel. Conflicting statements about who the statue represents are due to the fluidity of perceptions and the layers of meaning found in urban religious practices.

If Ólókūn and Òbiẹ̀mwẹ̀n are beneficial forces, Ògíùwú is destructive: Òvbí Òsà nẹ̀ òkúmàyán nẹ̀ ọ̀ rrié ẹ̀vbẹ̀ẹ̀ rrié íkpàkpá ("The merciless son of God who eats the kolanut and doesn't spare the shell"). A fate similar to Òbiẹ̀mwẹ̀n's seems to have befallen Ògíùwú. Before 1897, an Ògíùwú shrine stood next to the shrine of war in the old palace grounds. Human sacrifices were made there, to protect soldiers marching to battle, and again afterwards to celebrate victory. The encomium ìvbí Ògíùwú ("children of Death") referred to the Ẹ̀dó army. Ọ̀bá Ọ̀zòluà, the greatest warrior king, had a similar accolade. No images of Ògíùwú exist, because no artist dared draw the face of Death. Instead, Ọ̀fọ́ẹ̀ — Death's messenger — is depicted. Ọ̀fọ́ẹ̀'s head sprouts limbs which relentlessly pursue Death's victims. Because escape is impossible, Ọ̀fọ́ẹ̀ is called À-gùàn-á-í-họ́n ("[We] plead [but he] doesn't listen").

Two other major deities are hot and fiery, both beneficial and destructive: Ògún and Òsún. Ògún, the divinity of metal (especially iron), is identified with toolmaking and weapons, and serves as the patron of smiths, farmers, and soldiers. For protection from road accidents, taxi drivers and truckers carry Ògún's emblem in the form of a miniature hammer and forging tongs. Larger Ògún shrines consist of massive piles of scrap metal including chains and old engine parts. Nearly every household shrine has a small Ògún altar attached to it, because Ògún is the instrument of supernatural sanction:

Ẹ̀bọ̀ nẹ́ ọ̀ wẹ̀: "Ghá ré Ògún?"   The gods say "Who is Ògún?"
Úkpòkpò ọ̀ ré à yá gbẹ̀n yá àrò ẹ̀ré.   He is the cutlass which clears the
                                                      path to the shrine.

The Ẹ̀dó divinity Òsún, the power in leaves and plants, is partly distinct from the Yorùbá divinity Òṣun, whose core worship occurs on the banks of the Òṣun River in the Yorùbá-speaking town of Òṣogbo. The relationship between Ẹ̀dó and Yorùbá cosmology is complex, and Òsún may have historical and iconographic kinship with Òṣun. In her Yorùbá roles as the source of children and the patron deity of a city-state, however, Òṣun's closest correspondent in Ẹ̀dó religion is Ólókūn. Among the Ẹ̀dó, Òsún is never depicted in human form. Òsún shrines take the form of a large tree (èrhán) deep in the forest, surrounded by large pots full rainwater and leaves, the stuff of medicine. Òsún pots are also found in the male section of traditional homes; bathing in this water fortifies an individual for a journey or difficult task. Òsún also protects against an enemy in war. Long iron staffs topped by images of vultures and the chameleon (its body is believed to be poisonous to the touch) are powerful reminders that those under Òsún's protection defy death. The praise name of this staff is òsún-ní-giògiò ("boiling hot herbal medicine"). Such staffs were last used in 1947 by the Òtù-Ẹ̀dó, an Ẹ̀dó solidarity group, in public protests against the Yorùbá-based Ògbóní association which threatened the Ọ́bá's authority. In addition to Ólókūn, Ògún, and Òsún, the Ẹ̀dó have imported from Yorùbá-speaking area the divinity of divination (Ifá or Òrọ̀nmìlà), the gods' unpredictable messenger (Èṣù), and the god of thunder, Èsàngó (Ìsàgó in Ẹ̀dó). Ifá exists alongside its Ẹ̀dó equivalent, Ìhà Òmìnigbọ̀n. Ifá and Èṣù are linked: wherever there is an Òrọ̀nmìlà shrine, a shrine to Èṣù can be found in a niche near the doorway. Èṣù and Èsàngó are also linked, insofar as they seem to have jointly replaced Ògíùwú, who controls thunder as well as death (thunder is Death's voice). Like Ògíùwú, Èsàngó hurls thunderstones from the sky. Whenever prehistoric stone tools are unearthed, they are placed on shrines to stand for Èsàngó's and Ògíùwú's supernatural intervention.

There are myriad nature spirits. Ẹ̀zìzà, the bearded and hairy deity of the whirlwind, captures those who venture too far into the forest and, after putting them through a lengthy apprenticeship, returns them to the human world as his servants. Èsékú are dwarfs who inhabit lonely places; a hunter lucky enough to catch one would become instantly rich, but it is impossible to do so. Àdábì, the deity of the junction, straddles the boundary between this world and the next. A T, Y, or crossroads junction, is an energized point of contact between two realms (the numbers *3* and *4* are correspondingly powerful). A circled crossroads chalk design (ìghà-ẹ́dẹ́ "that divides the day"), evokes the allocation of time, the sharing of food, and protection from negative forces. There are also maleficent forces, to which portions of sacrificial kidney, liver, and intestines—ìzóbò, or "ambrosia for the gods"—are offered. Èníwánrẹ̀n-àsọ́n ("the elders of the night"), and Ìghèlé-èrínmwìn ("the founding fathers of the underworld") are ugly and grotesque monsters who snatch people and carry them off.

More immediate and accessible are numerous local spirits: divinized culture heroes (ìhện) and personifications of natural phenomena, such as rivers and hills. Some of these may have wider recognition, perhaps because they are associated with the reign of a powerful king. Òviá, for example, is a river spirit said to have lived at the time of Ọ̀bá Ẹ̀wuārè. Accused by jealous co-wives of having ìtèé, an illness of ceaseless menstruation, she was banished from the house and cried so much she turned into a river. Her cult is located in villages along the river that bears her name. Árúáràn, the giant half-brother of Ọ̀bá Ẹ̀sīgiè, is a stagnant lake at Ùdó, the stronghold from which he unsuccessfully contested the kingship. He is said to emerge from the lake, leaving telltale footprints that face in both directions. Ẹ̀mòtàn, whose monument adjoins the main market, was a trader who helped Ọ̀bá Ẹ̀wuārè attain the throne. Her shrine, originally the tree she turned into, now replaced by a statue, is visited on ceremonial occasions and has a caretaker from the palace.

The land itself is understood in metaphysical terms. Àrò-òtọ̀ ("the shrine of the ground") pinpoints the site of original habitation. The Ẹ̀dó refer to themselves as ìvbí òtọ̀, "children of the land" (but also ọviẹ̀n Ọ̀bá, "slaves of the king"). Animals, too, are not just food but also symbols of material and spiritual domains. One sacrifices and eats domestic animals like chickens, goats, and cows, thereby expressing domination over a portion of the created universe. Compared to these docile animals, wild creatures represent the hostility of untamed lands. Between these two categories is an intermediate zone on the fringe of the home or village, used for refuse including unclaimed corpses. This last is the haunt of scavengers like vultures and wild dogs.

Antelopes, bush-pigs, and cane rats (fondly called "grasscutters" in West Africa) are all wild animals, but so are leopards, elephants, viper, and giant pangolins. The latter creatures symbolize the power of legitimate authority. The leopard is fierce but graceful, an uncivilized force and a totemic emblem of royalty: only an Ọba may kill one. The elephant, bulky, blundering, and strong, represents chiefs and headstrong, powerful men. The Ọba owns the first tusk to hit the ground of every elephant killed in his kingdom. The Ọba's logo conjoins the leopard and the elephant, signifying the booty of war. The multicolored viper represents the gleaming wealth of the palace. Like the viper who waits for prey to come to it, the Ọba awaits his subjects' tribute. The giant pangolin, though docile, is deceptively strong, and may even overpower an attacking leopard. At rituals which dramatize their opposition to the palace, chiefs wear red garments cut to resemble pangolin skin.

The Òsún medicine staff, with its menacing silhouette of vultures, conveys these birds' injurious power. The cobra and mamba are poisonous; the chameleon is believed to be. The owl, cat, and dog are associated with the ability to transform themselves at night, and hence with witchcraft. They are dangerous because they blur the boundary between the human and animal realms. The ability to transform oneself into a night creature is the height of supernatural power. Witches and sorcerers send out their life force in the guise of a sinister animal.

The Èdó make a basic opposition between àgbọ̀n, the visible world, and erínmwìn, the world of spirits. Much energy is spent maintaining good relations with the deities and ancestors, and warding off bad fate and witchcraft. By regularly invoking the deities and ancestors, offering them food, gin, and kolanuts, and observing family taboos, one is assured of metaphysical support within the household. Extra protection is afforded by charms attached to door beams and thresholds, and by shrines located within the compound.

In coping with personal problems, the Èdó turn to the members of shrine groupings. Priestesses and priests are intermediaries: through trance and possession they convey messages from both sides of the divide. They develop their spiritual powers over many years, aided by medicinal and herbal treatments. The construction of shrines and the performance of rituals manifest divine inspiration. Although each practitioner has a unique approach to performance and image-making, a style is set for each divinity. Ólókūn adherents wear white àdàighó (ritually processed garments) and make abundant use of white chalk; Ògún's followers dress in red. To indicate Ògún's positive attributes, female worshippers may rub the left, or weaker, side of their faces with white chalk, but the dominant (right) side is smeared with red ochre. In a lifespan one is born under chalk (the moon), proceeds to camwood (the sun), and leaves with charcoal. Red always precedes black: no one suffers or dies without cause, and sickness or death usually result from a curse.

Fitting offerings to the "white" deities (Òsànóbùa, Ólókūn, and Òbiẹmwẹn) are themselves white: doves, cowries, coconut, white cotton, and china plates. Ólókūn accepts white fowl and goats. Ògún is served with red cockerels. Ògún kills, Òsún is hot medicine, Èsù brings confusion: a she-goat is too bland for these strong deities. Ògún's favorite food is dog: a taxi driver who runs over a dog rejoices in an instant offering! The hot deities also crave traditional fast foods, especially roasted yam and (red) palm oil. Several years ago, a spate of fatal road accidents prompted a temporary ban on the vending of these foods along the city's streets. The accidents were attributed to Ògún's craving for the foods that all but he were eating. Similarly, of Èsù it is said:

Èsù mú ìyèkè dé òwá, ọ nọ òvbúkhọ.   Èsù put his back against the house
                                                                           and asked for a he-goat.
À kpé ghè té ọ ghì mú ẹrò dé òdé vbò?   If he had put his face to the house,
                                                                           what then?

Oracular techniques range from èwàwà, which uses cowries and kolanuts, to Ìhà Òmìnìgbòn, a dense form of numerology which takes years to master. The 256 possible falls of the chain not only spell out the problem, they point to its solution. While there are many technical distinctions among diviners, priests, herbalists, and physicians—those skilled in the art of prophecy are not competent to perform circumcisions or set bones—all employ an overlapping knowledge of supernatural remedies, herbs, and natural medicaments.

Catering to the medicinal requirements of physicians and priests are kèmwín-kémwìn ("anything and everything") market stalls, where one finds a great variety of animals, vegetable, and mineral ingredients. Dried heads of eagles, vultures, bushrats, crocodiles, and monkeys;

lumps of chalk and mounds of cowries; jars full of dead, musty birds, leaves, and bark; divination implements; sacrificial items such as brass and iron cutouts in the shape of canoes, ladders, and vulture beaks; assorted bits and pieces of this and that which will be transformed, through the appropriate incantations, into amulets.

Ẹ̀dó State has as many as 20,000 traditional medical practitioners, yielding a ratio of 1:100, versus roughly 1:16,000 for medical doctors in the industrialized Occident. Government medical facilities not only do not compare in number, they intimidate nonliterate patients who find traditional healers more comforting and affordable. Malaria may be treated casually with remedies bought at a pharmacy or patent medicine store, and serious physical injuries may end up in an emergency room, but patients complaining of impotence, barrenness, infidelity, and exam or business failure hedge their bets by consulting both Western-trained and traditional practitioners, and by attending church as well as the shrine of one or more African divinities.

The most immediate contact with the other world is the spirits of the dead, the recently deceased and the collective ancestors, who meddle in human activities or give advice through dreams. Those who die unmarried or childless do not enter the spirit world; to become an ancestor one must have descendants. It is one's heir who builds one's ancestral shrine, which consists of a bell to summon the spirit from the other world and an ùkhùrhẹ̀—the carved wooden rattle staff of paternal authority. A new ùkhùrhẹ̀ takes its place among the staffs of those long deceased, and is used to ratify important decisions that affect the household. An adjacent room contains a shrine to deceased mothers, which includes a carved wooden hen, symbol of maternal affection, protecting her brood of chicks by enfolding them under her wings.

Anyone can make offerings to a dead parent or to the collective elders whose names are now forgotten. A householder makes annual sacrifices on behalf of all lineage members when he sacrifices to his head, seat of his judgment, luck, and character. The head is one of a triad of symbols for concepts of the person: ùhúnmwùn (the head or destiny), òbọ́ (the hand or acquisition), and ẹ̀hì (the spiritual guardian). While the Ẹ̀dó concept of the head recalls the Yorùbá idea of orí, their other personal cults are more like those of the Ìgbò. On the ìkẹ̀gà òbọ́ (shrine of the right hand), a large carved wooden cyclinder with clenched fist motif honors an individual's enterprise and achievement. Ìkẹ̀gà is a closed fist which says "I have caught it!"[5] The phrase Í mẹ́ òbọ́ ("I have no hand") is an admission of failure. When an animal is sacrificed at the installation of a chief, the celebrant receives its hand to show that he has achieved something noteworth in life. The Ẹ̀dó ẹhì is similar to the Ìgbò chí. The ẹhì and its living counterpart are two halves of a single being, indissoluably linked through fourteen successive reincarnations. The ẹhì remains in the spirit world as a guide and mentor for its living half and later and intercedes with the Creator after death, when the deceased spirit gives an accounting of its life and is allocated its lot (ùhìmwẹ̀n) in the next reincarnation.

Ẹ̀dó religious beliefs have remarkable coherence and vitality, despite centuries of missionary attack. One reason is the way they go beyond private, individual faith to sustain the whole social order. Thirty years after Nigerian independence, the Ọ́bá's political legitimacy remains unequalled in the eyes of the the Ẹ̀dó-speaking people. Ẹ̀dó religion, with its magnificent shrines and pageants, its diviners and herbalists, provides the public with social services which are scarcely available from state and federal ministries of Arts, Culture, Education, Health, and Welfare. As an oral tradition, Ẹ̀dó civilization is maligned and misrepresented by literates. The images in this book offer literate Nigerians and non-Nigerians alike an important bridge to the daily lived reality of the Ẹ̀dó-speaking people.

Notes

1. The Sokoto Caliphate pressed into the Yorùbá-speaking area throughout the eighteenth and nineteenth centuries; the Fulani gained control of Ìlọrin in 1820, undermining the Ọ̀yọ́ Empire. However, Islam did not displace indigenous Yorùbá culture; see Johnson 1921, Bíòbáků 1973, Abímbọ́lá (ed.) 1975.

2. See Forde and Jones 1950; Díkē 1956; Jones 1963; Alagoa 1972; Latham 1973; Áfíigbò 1981, 1987.

3. On stylistic evidence of the early Benin-Ífẹ̀ relationship, see Williams 1974.

4. See Bradbury 1973, Adéwọyè̀ 1977.

5. The corresponding figure on an Ìgbò shrine is called íkéngà; see Ọnwúéjíọ̀gwụ̀ (1981: 49).

References

Abímbọ́lá, W. *Ifá: An Exposition of Ifá Literary Corpus.* Ìbàdàn: Oxford University Press, 1976.

Abímbọ́lá, W. (ed.). *Yorùbá Oral Tradition.* Department of African Languages and Literatures, University of Ífẹ̀, Ilé-Ifẹ̀, 1975.

Adéwoyè, Ọ. *The Judicial System in Southern Nigeria 1854-1954.* London: Longman, 1977.

Áfáigbò, A. E. *Ropes of Sand; Studies in Ìgbo History and Culture.* Ìbàdàn: University Press Ltd, 1981.

Áfáigbò, A. E. *The Ìgbò and their Neighbours; Inter-Group Relations in Southeastern Nigeria to 1953.* Ìbàdàn: University Press Ltd, 1987.

Aigbe, E. I. *Ẹ̀dó-English Dictionary.* Lagos: Academy Press, 1985.

Agheyisi, R. N. *An Ẹ̀dó-English Dictionary.* Benin City: Ethiope, 1986.

Alagoa, E. J. *A Short History of the Niger Delta.* Ìbàdàn: Oxford University Press, 1972.

Ben-Amos, P. *The Art of Benin.* London: Thames and Hudson, 1980.

Bíobákú, S. (ed.). *Sources of Yorùbá History.* Ìbàdàn: Oxford University Press, 1973.

Bradbury, R. E. *The Benin Kingdom and the Ẹ̀dó-speaking Peoples of South-Western Nigeria.* Ethnographic Survey of Africa, pt. 13. London: International African Institute, 1957.

Bradbury, R. E. *Benin Studies.* Ìbàdàn: Oxford University Press, 1973.

Díkē̄, K. Ọ. *Trade and Politics in the Niger Delta, 1830–1885.* Ìbàdàn: Oxford University Press, 1956.

Èghárévbá, J. U. *Èkhérhé vb'Èbé Ítán Ẹ̀dó/A Short History of Benin.* Benin City: C.M.S., 1934; 2nd edition, Ìbàdàn University Press, 1960.

Èghárévbá, J. U. *The Benin Law and Custom.* Lagos: Service Press, 1946.

Ẹ́wẹ̄ká, Ena. *The Benin Monarchy.* Benin City: Bendel Newspapers, 1989.

Forde, D. and G. I. Jones. *The Ìgbò and Ìbìbìò-Speaking Peoples of South-Eastern Nigeria.* Ìbàdàn: Oxford University Press, 1950.

Johnson, S. *The History of the Yorùbás.* Lagos: C. S. S. Bookshops, 1921.

Jones, G. I. *The Trading States of the Oil Rivers.* Ìbàdàn: Oxford University Press, 1963.

Latham, A. J. H. *Old Calabar 1600–1891: The Impact of the International Economy upon a Traditional Society.* Ìbàdàn: Oxford University Press, 1973.

Melzian, H. *A Concise Dictionary of the Bini Language of Southern Nigeria.* London: Kegan Paul, 1937.

Ọ́nwụ́éjῑọ́gwụ̀. *An Ìgbò Civilization: Ǹrì Kingdom and Hegemony.* London: Ethnographica and Benin-City: Ethiope, 1980.

Williams, D. *Icon and Image; a Study of Sacred and Secular Forms of African Classical Art.* New York: New York University Press, 1974.

The Art of Ẹ̀dó Ritual

NORMA ROSEN

The Spirit World

Like many neighboring West Africa peoples, Ẹ̀dó-speakers with their capital in Benin City traditionally think of the world as existing on two planes. The self participates in everyday life in àgbọ̀n (the visible world), while ẹ̀rínmwìn (the world of the ancestors, which some people call heaven) is the home of one's personal guardian spirit (ẹ̀hì). Deities and spirits operate on both levels.

Moments before physically reincarnating into àgbọ̀n, you are said to perform a ceremony called Ùhímwẹ̀n ("Receiving destiny"). Kneeling beside your ẹ̀hì before Òsànóbùa the Creator, you declare what you will do on earth. That is why people appeal to their ẹ̀hì in both good circumstances and bad. There are no situations attributable to mere chance, that is, to luck, in either the positive or negative sense. One's success or failure is decided before birth. The events of one's life are predestined, and one is powerless to change them. Criminals, kings, the rich, and the poor all declare themselves in Heaven before entering the world. Ẹ̀hì-mwẹ́n-má ("My-ẹ̀hì-is-good") is a name given to a newborn child to show that it has come to do good deeds.

Ẹ̀dó people revere the passage of time: past, present, and future. Their ancestors' lives inform their present values, and they celebrate the future by raising children. Cognizant of their place in both worlds, àgbọ̀n and ẹ̀rínmwìn, they would not steal another person's property because someone would steal from them or from their children later on. In the same way, they revere the spiritual realm and believe in divine retribution.

Deities may help a person overcome daily obstacles and avoid accidents, but individual power resides in one's own head (ùhúnmwùn) and in one's ẹ̀hì with whom the head cooperates. One's head will curse or bless one's actions. Accordingly, when a traditional person is having problems, the first recourse is to placate the head and the ẹ̀hì, focusing on the sensitive place at the base of the back of the neck. This may be done on one's own or with the help of a priest or priestess. The same ritual applies to the Benin Kingdom as a whole: the annual Ìguẹ̀ Festival is a time of renewal for the Ẹ̀dó-speaking world in its entirety. At the core of Ìguẹ̀ is a series of palace sacrifices to the head of Ọ́bá, followed by sacrifices to the heads of all chiefs and commoners in their private homes.

"Serving the Head"

If a diviner advises you to "serve your head"—to worship it by ritual annointing—you can perform this ceremony yourself or have someone do it for you. A family group can also participate together.

You obtain a spotted guinea fowl, or else a white fowl which could be a pigeon or hen. You also need a coconut, ground white chalk (òrhuẹ̀), and some white or red kolanuts. The white coconut flesh is cut into thirty strips and one round piece. The round piece is laid on a white or glass plate, with the strips around it like a sunburst. The ground beneath the plate is washed and allowed to dry, then four parallel chalk lines are drawn and enclosed in a chalk circle roughly the size of a dinner plate. A spot of chalk is placed on your forehead, on the base of the back of your neck, and in front of each ear. The chalk symbolizes good news which the celebrant will hear: a head served with chalk brings rich blessings to its owner.

Prayers are made while chipping a lobe of kolanut into small bits with the thumbnail and placing these on the center of the head of each participant. The same process is repeated with a piece of the coconut. Next, a prayer is made while touching the fowl to the head. After the fowl is sacrificed, some of the blood is daubed on each person's forehead, in front of the ears and at the base of the back of the neck. (For a pregnant woman, blood is daubed on the shoulder instead of the head.) After the sacrifice, the bits of kola and coconut are dropped off the head and eaten from the right hand. Some of the coconut milk is sprinkled on the head, and then everyone sips from the remainder in the glass.

After "Serving the Head" comes "Going to Benin." The officiant takes the remaining coconut milk, the round piece of coconut, and a lobe of kolanut outside of the compound and leaves them there. While stepping out and returning, the officiant is greeted as if departing on a journey and arriving home. All this is done beneath the open sky. Then comes èníkàrò: prayers to the ancestors, with hands raised in the direction of the Ọ́bá's palace (ẹ̀guàè), giving chalk and coconut milk to the ground.

People serve their head at night and do not leave home again until morning. The sacrificed fowl is usually cooked the next day; the meat is shared among those who participated.

Ritual Art as Communication

In Ẹ̀dó religion, spiritual beings move between humans on earth and Òsànóbùa the Creator in heaven. Divinities such as Ólókūn (who governs conception), Òbiẹ̀mwẹ̀n (child-birth), and Ẹ̀zìzà (the whirlwind which carries medicinal forest herbs) come down to earth, where they are served by specialized priesthoods, in elaborate ceremonies that use ritual objects and musical instruments in dance and sacrifice.

The shrine and its òhện (priest or priestess) embody spiritual forces. Each line of worship has its essential tools; the choice and arrangement of objects in each shrine reflects the vision of its òhện, who may combine the skills and talents of artist, poet, dancer, musician, diviner, and herbal doctor.

Ì ghí mwẹ́n ọ̀bó óvbèhé oo.	I don't have any other diviner.
Ólókūn mwẹ́n né ọ̀ rrí ọ̀bó.	Ólókūn is my diviner.
Ì ghí mwẹ́n ọ̀bó óvbèhé oo.	I don't have any other diviner.
Ólókūn mwẹ́n né ọ̀ rrí ọ̀bó.	My Ólókūn is my diviner.
Ẹ̀zẹ̀ n'ùghègbè, dó ùghègbè!	River which is the mirror greetings to the mirror!
Dó ùghègbè né ọ̀ yó ẹ̀rínmwìn rré!	Greetings to the mirror that traveled to the spirit world and came back!

The idea of reflection is critical in Ólókūn worship. A river reflects the land and the sky, as well as anyone standing on its banks.

In Benin City, guilds practice ancient crafts of brass-casting, weaving, and carving. Many of the finished objects are used in the court of the Ọ́bá (Hereditary King). In every pattern in these traditional objects, a message is conveyed. To understand the craft process, one must translate the artists' messages in terms of their physical and cultural environment. Reverence for the past, combined with a constant need to communicate with the spirit world through tangible objects, inspires present-day Èdó artists.

A priestess will tell stories about Ólókūn, the divinity of the sea, to link her craft experience to the meaning of ceremonial dressmaking as a gesture of prayer. Every aspect of the creation of objects and drawn images for Ólókūn worship is a vehicle for communication with the spirit world.

<h2 style="text-align:center">Objects and Images of Ólókūn Worship</h2>

Òsànóbùa the Creator sent various deities—his children—to the world, to rule over nature and aid humanity. One of his children is Ólókūn, who resides in the sea. Preoccupation with water is a clue by which a person is called to Ólókūn priesthood. For those who dream about swimming in the ocean, Ólókūn initiation is advised. Nominal initiation lasts seven days; initiation as a priest or priestess takes fourteen.

All humans are endowed with special skills and a predestined individual assignment, prior to their arrival in the physical world. The task of religious practitioners, as artisans, is to create objects of carved wood and ivory, cast metal, clay, fabric, and leather, and charge them with spiritual power through songs and incantations. Working in a traditional religious group, an artisan invests an object with a life force above its utilitarian and decorative qualities. This process can be seen in the decoration of individual shrines and in the creation of related shrine objects such as àdáíghó.

Shrines, like costumes, are constructed and embellished by each priest or priestess. Interpretations of Ólókūn stories vary; so too does the approach of each òhẹ̀n to object-making and worship. The integrity and knowledge of the maker are respected just as much as their particular methods of worship. During divination or other ceremonies, four vertical chalk lines are drawn to show Ólókūn's ability to bring blessings straight from ẹ̀rínmwìn to àgbọ̀n. One song goes:

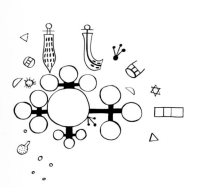

Various deities are represented in these designs including Ólókūn, god of fertility and wealth. The circular and crossroad images open the day. The ceremonial sword at the top suggests leadership, while the star, moon, ladder, and other drawings have cosmological significances.

Ólókūn yá y´uwà rré!   Ólókūn go and bring prosperity!

Yá yá yá o!   Bring, bring, bring!

Yá y´uwà rré!   Go and bring prosperity!

Yá yá yá o!   Bring, bring, bring!

But objects alone cannot reach the spirit world. It is humans who call Ólókūn with sweet songs, music, dance, costumes, prayers, and beautiful objects. With all these, we invoke Ólókūn's power for our benefit:

Ì rhiè ẹ́gógó rré,   I bring the bell,

Ì rhiè emàbà rré,   I bring the drum,

N´ì yá ghá gá òkún mwẹn,   That I can use to serve my Ólókūn,

È n´ì sẹ ẹdẹ́ ẹhì.   So that I can reach my ẹhì's day
                            [my time of reincarnation].

È á vbà ègbé,   We have met each other,

Èwọ̀è né àmẹ.   Residents of the water.

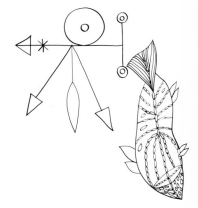

The large circle represents Òsànóbùa, the creator, while the perpendicular line ending in two circles suggests man's inability to thwart God's power. Ògún, deity of metal and war, is represented by three spears, and Ólókūn is depicted as the large fish.

This prayer invokes Ólókūn's protection, and implies that Ólókūn communicates with his worshippers through the voice of the bell. At another level we understand that, just as a bell can't ring without a clapper, there would be no children in the world without Ólókūn:

Ọmọ, ẹ́i wú ázà.   Ázà-bell, don't lose the child.

Ọmọ, ẹ́i wú éróró.   Éróró-bell, don't lose the child.

Ólókūn ghẹ́ giè ọmọ wú mwẹn.   Ólókūn, don't let me lose the child.

No one who would enjoy life would oppose God, just as no one willingly eats an unsalted meal:

Èrhẹn ghí mú vbe ẹ̀zẹ̀   A river cannot catch fire

Sìrà ẹgbó.   In the presence of the forest.

À í kp´ítán yé ọ̀nà

Ọ̀mwàn n´ọ kp´ítán yé ùmwẹ̀n,

Òkòró ọ̀ ghá ré.

Òsà n´érhá mwẹ̀n.

No one can dispute this.

Whoever says something against salt,

It is bland meals that he will eat.

God my father.

As people faithfully worship Ólókūn, they are correspondingly rewarded:

Ólókūn, lá òwá dò ré!

Ẹ̀zẹ̀ ghí lé ẹguàè,

Íyé o o o,

Ẹ̀zẹ̀ ghí lé ẹguàè.

Ólókūn, come inside!

The river does not run from the palace,

Oh my mother,

The river does not run from the palace.

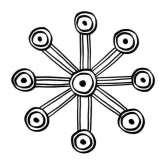

Ìghà-ẹ̀dẹ́, "that divides the day," is a simple cross design with circles. Its meanings are many: the transmission of messages to and from the other world, sharing of food among the deities, allocation of ritual time, detection of physical ailments, and the division of earthly and spiritual realms.

Chalk images may be either sifted or painted in shrines. I have yet to see two identical designs, though the symbols are often similar. Likewise, each priest's perception of Ólókūn varies to some degree. One important symbol is ìghà-ẹ̀dẹ́, the junction (àdà) where two roads meet.

In Ólókūn worship, as in other branches of Ẹ̀dó religion, every ritual and every object or icon has a specific meaning and contributes to the success of the entire process. This is quite different from most aesthetic object-making in the West, where the link between artisan and object is severed after the "making" process is done.

Ólókūn's ceremonial objects, dresses, and iconography are ritually charged with power through the use of various herbs and leaves as well as sacrificial offerings and prayers. There is a close relationship between physical objects and verbal communication. The verbal and the visual are interdependent. Every action, every object, and every chalk drawing on the floor of the shrine, is a vehicle for prayer. The chalk designs drawn at a shrine before an afternoon dance (ùgiè àvàn) will probably be erased by vigorous dancing. The act of drawing is a form of communication between the hand of the priest and these deities, but the physical image serves only as a footprint of the spirit and may be wiped out by other ritually inspired footprints.

Ceremonies range from individual prayers to elaborate sacrifices and astonishing divination dances which last from afternoon till night. In ritual, the other world is near at hand. As prayers are offered by devotees and priests, vast energies flow back and forth between àgbọ̀n and ẹrínmwìn.

The Ólókūn Afternoon Dance Ceremony

The afternoon ceremony (ùgiè àvàn) for the worship of Ólókūn follows a cycle of six phases:

1. introduction
2. possession and divination
3. sacrificial offering

4. intermediate resting songs
5. culmination
6. end resting songs

Before exploring these stages in detail, some background will be presented.

The traditional week contains four days, which in Ẹ̀dó are called Ẹ̀kì Ọ́bá ("The Ọ́bá's Market"), Ẹ̀kẹ́nākà, Ẹ̀kì Àgbàdò ("Àgbàdò Market"), and Ẹ̀kẹ́n. A specific deity (or deities) is worshipped on each day. Ẹ̀kẹ́n, spiritually charged, is called the "native Sunday": no farmwork is done on Ẹ̀kẹ́n, which is reserved for the worship of Ògún. Ólókūn, the owner of fertility and wealth, is associated with the marketplace and is accordingly worshipped on either Ẹ̀kì Ọ́bá or Ẹ̀kì Àgbàdò.

In any shrine, prior to any act of worship, the sacred space must be prepared. Before drawings are made anywhere, the entire compound is swept. Proverbially, a person who sweeps is never lost in the action of sweeping. Ò kpòló úghè í kpòló wìí. ("An arena sweeper doesn't sweep and get lost," that is, organization brings clarity of mind.) The inside of the shrine is then purified, including the altar with its medicinal pots, cast brass bells, moulded clay figures, and other sacred objects. Purification is performed with specific medicinal items: àfọ́ leaves soaked in a water and chalk mixture with cowries and coins; ẹ̀hiẹ̀n Ẹ̀dó ("Benin pepper" or black peppercorns, also called "alligator" pepper); and an eggshell from a nonhybrid ("non-agriculture") chicken, tied to the end of a broomstraw. Purification is performed, first by the Chief Priestess or Priest, and then by anyone entering the shrine.

Special seating is given to elders (èdiọ́n). If the shrine has an interior dance floor, members are seated there according to their title and seniority of initiation. Responsibilities are allocated by these titles, which the Chief Priest assigns while in trance. Some examples:

Ègbé ("Body") dresses the Chief Priest(ess) with medicines and àdàíghó prior to a ceremony, and accompanies the Chief Priest(ess) onto the dance floor.

Àghọnghọn ("Shadow") is always by the side of a Chief Priest(ess) who is either divining in a trance state or leaving the dance floor. Àghọnghọn ọmwàni ẹ sẹ ọmwàn raè. ("A person's shadow never goes away.")

Èhì ("Guardian angel") escorts the Chief Priest(ess) in all activities. This title can be given to an adult child of the Chief Priest(ess), since a child won't mislead its parent. For the same reason, the ẹhì title may also be given to a wife of the Ọba. Èhì ọmwàn ọ sú ọmwàn né à ì ná dé. ("It is your ẹhì that leads you so that you won't fall.")

Èhọ ("Ears") repeats questions from others, as the Chief Priest(ess) speaks in trance. After the ceremony, Èhọ confers with the Chief Priest(ess) and members about statements made in trance. Also, news of any type heard by Èhọ is reported to the Chief Priest(ess).

Prior to dressing for ritual dance, an òhện (priest or priestess) may bathe with a medicinal preparation. Àkpálódè (protective medicinal belts) may be worn under the garments. A medicine called ókìn-í-kín-ìkián ("dizziness-can't-catch-a-fly") can be incised on the back of the hands, beside the armpits or beside the eyes. In a whirling dance, the hands are wiped from under the armpits across the eyes, so that no matter how vigorous and quick the spinning motion, the vision clears immediately. Applied only once, the medicine stays in the body.

A goatskin fan (èzúzù) helps to maintain balance during vigorous dancing and whirling steps and is also used like the baton of an orchestra conductor. Ìghẹ̀gàn ẹwàẹ̀n, representing Ólókūn's wisdom, is a medicinal pendant made of cowries, red coral beads, blue ìgbàghọn beads, and a small brass bell (ìghẹ̀gàn). The style of tying the pendant varies with the spiritual lineage of the Chief Priest(ess).

Before the ceremony, the shrine of Òsànóbùa the Creator—always located outdoors—is served with ẹvbẹ̀ẹ̀ (ritual kola nuts) and chalk. At most shrines, wine is also used, but Òsànóbùa rejects alcohol (Òsà wùá àyọ́n). Members purify themselves before going inside. Shoes are left at the door, heads are bare.

The head is touched to the floor in front of the altar, then the arms are raised with clenched fists in salutation. As prayers are offered, the ázà (a square, cast bell) is rung in invocation. With the back facing the altar, the same gesture is offered again, for the spirits see all sides of a person.

Ólókūn's musical instruments are the following:

Úkúsẹ̀—a calabash covered with a net of beads, played mainly by women.
Èmà—a goatskin drum made from a hollowed log. In Ólókūn ceremonies, *èmà* are played in pairs.
Ẹ́gógó—a bell made of forged iron sheets and beaten with a wooden stick.

Seven introductory songs are sung by the members to call the spirits into the shrine. These songs are slow and very melodic, accompanied by úkúsẹ̀ alone. (At this stage, drums and bells are not used.)

Érhá ghí diẹ̀n íkhímwìn,	There is no tree elder than íkhínmwîn
	[the first tree in the world],
Òìsà ọ̀ ré ọdiọ́n.	God is first by seniority.

Possession, Divination, and Proverbial Advice

As the ceremony progresses to the next stage, the atmosphere crackles with excitement. Except for the seated instrumentalists, all the members form a circle. The Chief Priest(ess) enters, accompanied by any elders (èdiọ́n) who are not already present. Any member, before performing, first greets the altar, then greets the other members. Each fully initiated Priest(ess) greets the performer with raised arms, touching forearms and elbows, then backs and the backs of the arms, in an upright gesture. As the performer passes each member and acknowledges every Priest(ess), he or she is greeted Íyárrè! ("Go and return safely [from the spirit world]!").

A dancer's legs, face, and neck may be rubbed with powdered chalk. Someone is designated to follow the dancers and throw powdered chalk and salt at their feet. The performer may divine or sing, giving advice in proverbial form. A dancer who becomes possessed will jump up and shout "Ẹ́yọ̀!" or tremble violently. Someone in trance may dance

The diamond pattern of beauty and the dotted fan are for Ólókūn, god of harmony, wealth and children. The lightning darts and bow and arrow suggest Èsàngó (Isago), deity of thunder.

Drawn in powdered camwood, charcoal, and shifted white chalk, the images include the sun and its shadow, the half moon, stars, and the powerful crossroads, the means by which messages travel between worlds.

vigorously for forty-five minutes or longer. Afterwards, a priest or priestess may repeat messages from the spirit world.

While in trance, the dancer signals with a fan to increase or decrease the drum tempo. The dancer can stop the drums by touching them, to introduce new songs as different deities approach the floor. When different deities enter the dance floor, the drummers know by changes in the dancer's steps, posture, and facial expression. In full Ólókūn rhythms, the body moves in balanced harmony with vine-like and snake-like arm movements, then with twirls and spins. The hands are graceful and expressive mirrors of flowing water. Bells and úkúsẹ̀ predominate in Èsàngó dance, which emphasizes sharp, oscillating head and body motions. (A lot of neck strength is required.) Ògún's acrobatic dance rolls back and forth in a warrior's stance, while the hands make aggressive gestures. A fast rhythm of drums and bells is featured. Èzìzà dances in fast spinning turns, skipping on one foot or whirling symmetrically from clockwise to counter-clockwise. Instead of a fan, a fly-whisk (ùgbùdìàn) is used. Bells predominate.

Here are some songs which accompany the dance:

Ólóí n´amẹ̀,   Queen of the water,
Ùgìè ímà yé.   We are in the midst of ceremony.
Ọ̀bó wẹ̀ ˝Dó!˝   The diviner says "Greetings!"
Ọ̀bó ˝Dó!˝   The diviner says "Greetings!"

Mú òkpé èrhán,   Carry a big tree,
Ẹ̀hóhò mú òkpé èrhán,   A breeze doesn't carry off a big trees,
N´ù zẹ́ ẹ̀ré òbọ́.   You leave it alone.

Kù mẹ́ ghè,   Dance for me,
Kù mẹ́ ghè,   Dance for me,
Ùghègbè N´ébō, kù mẹ́ ghè!   Mirror, the white person, dance for me!
Ùghègbè N´ébō, kù mẹ́ ghè!   Mirror, the white person, dance for me!
L´úghè yó l´úghè rré,   To and fro in the town square,
Ẹ̀zìzà n´ọ̀bọ́.   Goes Ẹ̀zìzà, the physician.

Ògún mwẹn, Ògún wẹ ″Dó!″   My Ògún, Ògún says "Greetings!"
Ògún n´èrhẹn mwẹn   Ògún my fire
N´à´yá gb´ugbó,   With which we farmed,
N´à yá gb´ógò.   With which we clear last year's farm.

Òsà n´èrhá mwẹn.   God my father.
Òrhọ dé, ùyùnmwùn rré.   Rainy season approaching, dry season going.
Ì ghí mwẹn ọmọ né à zẹ yó ẹrinmwìn.   I have no child to send to the spirit world.

Ì hé kò dé,   I am coming gradually,
Ì yá àgbọn rh´ulẹ.   I am not headed for this world in haste.

À í ghí gbé Ọbá n´àmẹ.   Nobody destroys the King of the water.
Ì vba Ọbá n´àmẹ mwẹn.   I take refuge in the King of the water.
À tá mú ẹ̄ ré, ì wà ùnú mwẹn.   Prophetic speech comes forth
                from my mouth.

Some say Ògún descended from heaven to earth on a chain. The spears, swords, and arrows indicate his ability to open the path or clear the road.

Culmination

At last, the dancer may ritually serve drink to the nearby road junction, leaving the floor momentarily with an escort (usually the Òdìbò). The rhythm slows, as all deities are mentioned prior to the exit. Upon return to the circle, the dancer sings praises to the deities for having accepted the gift. The dancer cues the members that the spirit is leaving the dance floor to return to the spirit world, leaving the physical body for its owner:

Ì rrìè òwá mwẹn n´íbò.   I am going to my house, fellow worshippers.
Àrò ghí miẹ òdẹ ìyèkè,   Your eyes should not see your back,
Àrò ghí miẹ òdẹ ìyèkè.   Your eyes should not see your back.

As this song is raised, the Òdìbò and others throw powdered chalk in a line to lead the dancer off the floor and into a secluded room to cool down and return into the physical world.

As each individual dances, the Chief Priest(ess) scatters paper money at their feet; when the Chief Priest(ess) dances, members may reciprocate, especially during the annual festival. The Chief Priest(ess), coming last, divines for the members while in trance.

Endpoint

Égbọ̀ songs are for resting, after the dancer has retired into seclusion. The lyrics thank the dancer for being brilliant, and praise the deities' power to act in the physical, visible realm. Égbọ̀ songs relieve the tension of a long period of trance, and segue into the next performance or an intermission. They are slow, melodic and generally acapella, similar in pace to the introductory songs. An example:

Ọbẹ́ ùgiè ènái mwẹ́n,	Greetings, my Lord,
	on the ceremonial occasion,
Ènái mwẹ́n n´ẹ̀hì mwẹ́n!	My lord who is my guardian angel!
À yá ghá yá mẹ́,	Whatever I am given as a gift,
À mẹ́ ghí mẹ́ mwẹ́n ré.	No one should take from me.

This song also concludes our discussion of Ẹ̀dó ritual art, which achieves its purpose in bridging the spiritual and material worlds.

Ọ̀khẹ̀rrẹ̀ mán vbà òtọ̀ẹ í ghí mọ́.

If a palm tree doesn't cooperate with the ground,
it won't bear fruit.

*Divine
Inspiration*

45

Dr. Paula Ben-Amos first drew me to Benin studies. Dr. Joseph Nevadomsky and Professor S. I. Wangboje arranged my teaching appointment at the University of Benin in 1983–86. This project was supported in part by a grant from the University of Benin Committee on Research and Publication.

Throughout my stay in Benin City, many people gave generously of their time, knowledge and other resources. In particular, I would like to thank my research assistants Mr. Pius Guobadia and Mr. Agbọnifo Ovenseri; my research advisor, Mr. Ikponmwosa Ọsẹmwẹgie; Chief Nosakhare Isekhure, the Isekhure of Benin, for advice on ritual matters; Dr. Rebecca N. Agheyisi for linguistic advice; Igiohẹn Ebibierhen, Amalawa Orumwense; Babalawo Imafidọn Azaigueni; Ohẹn Ukhurebo; Igiohẹn Ọba Amẹ and Madame Aigbovia; my husband, Chief Priest Anthony Evbagharu Ogiemwanye, N'Ohẹn Ẹziza, who supports my spiritual quest with his love and profound wisdom; as well as Madame Igbinosa Igbinedion, Iye Ukpo Uri, Ohẹn Igbaghon, Irene Kubeyinje, and all the members of Ẹzẹ N'Ughegbe Shrine.

My other main consultants in Ẹdo, Ọyọ and Ondo States of Nigeria were the following. Igiohẹn Ighomo Ogbebo, Ohẹn Igbinosa Eresọnyẹ, Pa Onaiwu Ugiagbe, Ohẹn Ebigbon, Chief Ẹhidiaduwa Onaghinọ, Igiohẹn Uyiẹkpẹn, Madame Agbọnavbare, Ohẹn Felicia Osunde, Babalawo Joseph Osaghae, Ohẹn Madam Igbinosa, David Ọmọregie, Ohẹn-Akpowa N'Odibo, Ohẹn Ogun No Taimwin, Ohẹn-Ebose Enogheghase, Ohẹn-Imene'N'Okpogie Enogheghase, The Ediọn of the Urhonigbe Shrine, Mr. Idemudia Uwugiaren, Eze-Iyi Ayibor Okotiebor Opute. Isele Mary Anị-Oji Opute. Babalawo J. Dada, Ile-Ifẹ, Chief Awotọla Ojo, Adagbọn-Awo of Ogbaga, Igiohẹn Ọbazenu.

Since 1984, I have been very fortunate to live close to some of these priests, priestesses and artisans, and to be accepted as a student and a daughter by some of their families. Over many months of study, I began to see how Ẹdó people's traditional crafts anchor their beliefs. To interpret this religious foundation in objects, images and performances has been particularly fascinating to me.

— *Norma Rosen*

Photographs from
Benin City, Nigeria

Devotees at an Ólókūn ceremony, draped in àdàíghó (ritual dresses) and carrying èzúzù (leather fans) for dancing.

Babaláwo (Ifá divination priest) Ímáfídǫn Ázàìgùèní, with his divining chain.

The various shrine objects of this Ólókūn priestess are metaphysical tools through which Ólókūn passes messages into the visible world. The chalk drawing under the chair marks a sacred location and greets Ólókūn.

Madame Àgbọ̀návbārè, seated before her Ólókūn shrine. Her àdàíghó, or ritual garment, is decorated with cowrie shells, a traditional form of currency and a symbol of wealth.

The Èsàngó shrine of Madame Àgbọ̀návbārè. White represents purity and joy, red means sacrifice
and blood. The lightning strikes on the back wall represents Èsàngó in action.

Èdíọ́n (elders) of the Òbiẹ́mwẹ̀n shrine.

Ẹ̀mwẹ̀ n'érhá mwẹ́n khà mà
Mwẹ́n m'í mẹ́ ghá yá yí.
Ẹ̀dẹ́ ghè ghá rhiè, ọ̀tá ghá gbé èkó ègbé.

It is the words my father tells me
that I will always believe.
When you become older, you will understand
the inner feelings of others.

54

Òfóè carries messages to the inhabitants of earth on behalf of Ògíùwú the Deity of Death. For Òfóè day and night are the same, so he has two sets of arms and legs. As Òfóè can appear suddenly, at any time or place, Death may come suddenly, without warning and perhaps by accident. Death chooses victims regardless of age, health, or economic conditions. Òfóè may be moulded or carved in shrine doors.

Ólókūn priestess Ilerhunwa Ibude standing between the guardian of the shrine and a wall figure of Òfóè, the messenger of death.

Úyìèkpẹ̀n, Ìgìòhẹ̀n of Ògún wearing àkpálódè, leather amulets that protect one against danger.

Úyìèkpèn's shrine to Ògún, the god of metal, toolmaking, and weapons. It contains protective medicinal belts and canes, leaves, and other herbal preparations.

Ògún first came to the world in the shape of Ùmọ̀mọ̀, a big iron rod. Because essential tools did not yet exist, Ògún set fire to the òkpàghà tree (Pentaclethra macrophylla), melted Ùmọ́mọ̀ in the flame, and produced iron tools — machetes, knives, hoes, digging sticks, spades, shovels, and spears, etc. Ever since, blacksmiths have ùmọ́mọ̀ in their workshops, recalling Ògún's first appearance in the world.

(top right) The shrine represents Ògún as a hunter.
(bottom right) Ògún shrines consist of piles of scrap iron, including chains and old engine parts.

Òsún is the power in leaves and plants. Shrines take the form of trees deep in the forest, large pots of rainwater, and leaves, the stuff of medicine. Bathing in this medicine fortifies an individual for a dangerous journey.

Long iron staffs topped by images of vultures are powerful reminders that those under Òsún's protection defy death.

Children dressed for Ólókūn (in white) and Èsàngó (in red) before an Ólókūn shrine.

Ólókūn priestess, elder of the Ẹ̀zẹ̀ N'Ùghẹ̀gbè shrine, wearing the "wisdom of Ólókūn" pendant and holding an áza̒ bell, used for summoning spirits.

Guardians protecting the entrance to the shrine.

Clay effigies of Ólókūn, his attendants, and guardians. Mirrors symbolize water and mediate trance possession to the other world.

Ọ̀rọ́nmìlà, divinity of divination.

Twin figures with a wooden carving of òrìrrì, the electric eel.

Ùhúnmw'Ídùmwùn shrine, one of four national shrines to Ólókūn in the Èdó Kingdom, a privilege granted by Ọ́bá Ẹ́wúarè in the fifteenth century in recognition of the community's assistance against other contenders for the throne.

Madame Ìgbìnòsà Érésọ̀nyẹ̀ at the entrance to her Èsàngó shrine.

Fraternal twins, Táíwò and Kẹ̀hìndé, dressed for Èsàngó worship.

The central objects on these Èsàngó shrines are thunderstones.

Èsàngó controls thunder and death.

Priestess Ìdúhọ̀n of Èsàngó.
Only a fully initiated òhẹ̀n can wear red parrot feathers.

Òsàgìẹ̀dẹ́, priest of Ẹ̀zìzà, god of the whirlwind.

Priest Òsàgìèdẹ́'s shrine to Òsún. The candles, kolanuts, and chalk in the foreground
are typical offerings to this deity.

79

Ẹ̀zìzà travels throughout the world day and night. Air is everywhere in every land. There is no corner of the house where the breeze doesn't reach. Ẹ̀zìzà the whirlwind is everywhere. He lives in the forest and makes all the herbs and medicinal plants into active medicines for healing, protection, and childbirth.

Ẹ̀zìzà gié ẹ̀bò sẹ́,   Ẹ̀zìzà, let the medicine be potent,
Ẹ̀zìzà gié ẹ̀bò w'ẹ̀gbé.   Ẹ̀zìzà, let the medicine work in the body.

Ẹ̀zìzà priest Odenwingie before his shrine.

The shrine to Creator God is an íkhínmwîn tree, "the oldest tree in the world."
Offerings of kola, chalk, coconuts, and pumpkins are found at its base.

Priest of Ẹ̀zìzà and Priestess of Ólókūn standing in front of an Èsù shrine. Èsù, the trickster,
is a messenger for the Yorùbá deity Ifá.

Finger-painted in white chalk, the fish is a symbol of Òlókūn.

Ladders are a symbol of spiritual ascension and aspiration in Òlókūn worship.

Mr. Lawrence Ọ̀mọ́rūyì, Priest of Èsàngó.

Priestesses of Èsàngó Helen Òghámā and Rose Ọ̀mọ́rūyì.

An Ólókūn priestess, wearing ìvié (coral beads) and an ìghẹ̀gàn ẹ̀wàẹ̀n, a pendant representing Ólókūn's wisdom.

Madame Àígbòvíá, a high priestess, dressed for her annual Èsàngó ceremony and holding
a medicine gourd. Red symbolizes this deity of lightning and thunder.

Individual power resides in one's own head (ùhúnmwùn) and in one's guardian spirit (ẹhì)
with whom the head cooperates. One's head will curse or bless one's actions.

Madame Òsúndé and her daughter, in her shrine to Òbiẹmwẹ̀n, protector of pregnancy and childbirth.
The chalk drawing depicts àbébè, a river fern used to stop bleeding and prevent miscarriage.

Sú mwẹ́n, sú mwẹ́n, ẹ̀hì.	Lead me, lead me, guardian spirit.
Sú mwẹ́n, sú mwẹ́n, ẹ̀hì mwẹ́n.	Lead me, lead me, my guardian spirit.
Su mwẹ́n, su mwẹ́n, ẹ̀hì.	Lead me, lead me, guardian spirit.
Ẹ̀hì ọmwàn ọ̀ sú ọmwàn né à i ná dé.	It is your ẹ̀hì that leads you so that you won't fall.

Priest surrounded by children at his shrine.

No tabuleiro da Baiana tem vatapá, ôi, caruru, mungunzá, ôi, tem umbu p'rá Ioiô.

Se eu pedir, você me dá o seu coração, seu amor de Iaiá?

No coração da Baiana tem sedução, ôi, canjerê, ilusão, ôi, candomblé.

"P'rá você juro por Deus, pelo Sinhô do Bonfim, quero você Baianinha, inteirinha p'rá mim."

Sim, mas depois, o que será de nós dois?

Teu amor é tão fugaz e enganador.

Tudo já fiz, fui até num canjerê p'rá ser feliz, meus trapinhos juntei com você.

Sim, mas depois, vai ser mais uma ilusão.

Que no amor quem governa é o coração.

On *Baiana*'s tray, there is *vatapá*, hey, *caruru*, *mungunzá*, hey, and *umbu* for you, Massa.[1]

If I ask you, will you give me your heart, your love for Missy?

In *Baiana*'s heart, there is seduction, oh, *canjerê*, illusion, oh, *candomblé*.[2]

"To you I swear to God, to the Lord of the Happy Ending,

   I want you Little Baiana, all for me."

Yes, but afterwards, what will happen to the two of us?

Your love is so fleeting and deceitful.

I've done everything, I even went to a *canjerê* to be happy and joined my things with yours.

Yes, but afterwards, it's going to be one more illusion.

Because in love, what rules is the heart.

Candomblé
Is Religion-life-art

ZECA LIGIÈRO

The song by Ary Barroso, recorded in the 1930s by Carmen Miranda, portrays the black Bahian street vendor—the baiana—who hawks the favorite foods of the orixá—the Yorùbá gods. From this stereotype, Miranda created her trademark "made in Brazil" character, complete with rolled head-tie, embroidered blouse, starched layered skirts, and necklaces of figas and patuás. In this role, she demonstrated the Brazilian transformation and adaptation of African elements. However, while the lyrics praise the seductive power of the baiana and her food, they also associate Candomblé with deception and danger. African elements are absorbed, but their origins are stigmatized.

Although African culture is found throughout Brazil, it is most concentrated in Salvador, the state capital of Bahia. Until the legal abolition of slavery in 1888, Salvador was strongly linked to the Bight of Benin through the massive importation of slaves. Thereafter, the connection was maintained by other forms of trade, especially in Brazilian tobacco. Today, Salvador is the center of many self-described "Afro-Brazilian" religious and artistic groups. For more than a century, African traditions have been preserved in the assentamento (sacred vase) of Candomblé. During the slaving period, descendants of different linguistic groups from the Bight of Benin began to practice their respective religious cults under the same roof: the terreiro (Candomblé shrine house). Thus, the African presence was validated, as African religions, languages, myths, music, dance, and songs were maintained.

Even so, African traditions changed in Salvador. As a form of religious resistance,

97

Candomblé created a syncretic pantheon from African oral traditions. Pages 146, 163, 167, 169, show that divinities worshipped in different African states have their assentamentos side by side in the collective peji (altars) of Brazil. Constant attacks by the Church forced Candomblé practitioners to adopt Catholic saints as disguises for their own deities. And when Candomblé spread to other Brazilian territories, it came under new influences, both Amerindian and European. From these successive transformations emerged rituals and performances which — though filled with ancient African lore — were new and eclectically Brazilian.

Nine Rolls of Tobacco for a Slave

Portuguese aristocrats carved up the land of Brazil into hereditary domains. The discovery of gold and precious stones made these tracts quite valuable. Sugar cane was also grown with great success. However, the profits of all these enterprises depended upon slave labor. Under the harsh yoke of slavery, the indigenous Americans (called Indians) fell ill or committed suicide, and the Church soon interceded in their favor. So Portugal turned to Africa for its human labor power. During four centuries, countless Africans were transported to serve in Brazil. Under the worst conditions, they cleared the forests of the Atlantic coast, dug gold in Minas Gerais, grew sugar in the Northeast and tobacco in Bahia. They also performed domestic work: cooking, cleaning, and childcare.

For the Portuguese, a single color — black — named all Africans, but Brazilian slaves came from many different regions. In his great historical work *Fluxo e Refluxo do Tráfico de Escravos entre o Golfo de Benin e a Bahia de Todos os Santos*, Pierre Verger divides the Bahian slave trade into four periods according to the main sources of human cargo:

Guinea	latter sixteenth century
Molembo (now Angola) and Congo	seventeenth century
Gold Coast (now Ghana, Togo)	first three-fourths of the eighteenth century
Bight of Benin	1770–1850
(now Republic of Benin, Nigeria)	(including clandestine slave trade)

Portuguese ships brought the first Africans to Brazil in 1538, in the classic triangular pattern. In African ports, European merchandise was exchanged for slaves, who were sold in Bahia for gold, which was carried to Lisbon to buy more merchandise. But in 1637 the Dutch captured Castelo de São Jorge da Mina (in the present-day country of Ghana, where it is called El Mina), just as the demand for labor rose in the silver mines of Bahia, the gold and diamond mines of Minas Gerais, and the sugar plantations of the north and northeast. Just four Gold Coast ports remained: Grand Popo, Ouidah, Jaquim, and Apá. Further, the Dutch only let the Portuguese import tobacco, the production of which was centered in Bahia. The Portuguese themselves banned "third-class" tobacco (consisting of small and broken leaves) from import into Portugal: what was not consumed in Brazil was sent to Africa. Before export, it was processed with sugarcane syrup, adding a special aroma. Verger calculates that in 1750 a slave could be bought for nine rolls of sweetened, third-class tobacco.

Portuguese trade in Gold Coast ports was further hindered by Dutch boycotts and high taxes (about 10 percent), and by the fall of the fortress of Ouidah to the king of "Dahomey" (Àgbòmé). In the late eighteenth century, Portuguese slave traders increasingly turned east to the Bight of Benin—especially to Porto Novo, Badagry (Àgbádárìgì), and Lagos (then called Onim). From 1815, when Britain prohibited slave trading north of the Equator, the Portuguese opened new routes to Molembo (now called Angola) and the Congo. At the same time, they used various strategies to keep taking slaves from the Bight of Benin: a passport would be issued for Molembo, but the ship would stop in Porto Novo along the way.

Monique Augras notes a correspondence between the massive importation to Bahia of Nagô (that is, Yorùbá speakers), beginning in 1830, and the fall of the Yorùbá Empire of Òyó in 1835. The importation of many prisoners from Òyó's higher social classes, especially Ifá priests, certainly added fuel to African cultural continuations in Salvador. Above all, according to Verger, the relatively recent and concentrated arrival of Yorùbá speakers in Bahia explains their strong contemporary influence.

Resistance of African Culture

In 1741, the Catholic Church decided that the Negro has a soul. In the Papal bull *Immensa Pastorum Principis*, Pope Benedict XIV stated that although they were heathens, Negroes could nevertheless be converted just like other races. Yet the Church never suspected that

Africans had their own concept of the soul, a concept which explained their unyielding faith, deep philosophy, and complex rituals. Among the different linguistic groups, the Yorùbá, Angolans, and Jeje (Dahomeans) left an outstanding legacy of concepts for the living forces of nature in divine form: orixá, inkisi, and vodun.

Gisèle Cossard remarks that "in Africa, individuals who become detribalized and leave the forest to try their luck in the city are quick to let go of their past, abandon their traditional beliefs and adopt new customs." During this adaptation phase, both Islam and Christianity "represent progress and social promotion which favors daily increasing contact with European civilization." Inversely in Brazil, slaves "held on to their memories and endured their suffering through faithfulness to their origins" (1970: 1).

Both nostalgia and rebellion were present in early nineteenth-century Bahia. Slave revolts were innumerable, and there were many isolated attempts to organize quilombos (free settlements of runaway Africans). The fight for freedom unified the descendants of traditionally rival nations. Aware of the danger this posed, the owners began to let slaves meet on Sundays—under supervision and divided by language and nation—to dance and sing with drums (see Rodrigues 1932: 234–35). But instead of deepening the conflicts between linguistic groups, such drumming and dancing promoted fraternization. Cascudo (1965: 136), citing Sarmento, notes the Angola/Congo origin of the batuque. The batuque was a major social catalyst enabling various linguistic groups and nations to join in peaceful, nonliturgical celebration. The same thing happened some decades later in the first Candomblés in Salvador.

Persecution of the Candomblés continued even after the end of slavery. Rodrigues notes a headline in *Gazeta do Povo*, August 16, 1905: "At a Candomblé. Things of sorcery, madness and death". The story describes a man who fell ill at a ceremony and died some hours later in his home. He "had been retired due to his state of insanity, resulting from his initiation into things of sorcery." The newspaper then goes on to comment on the "proliferation of the Negroes' religious practices":

What stands out admirably is the extraordinary resistance and vitality of these beliefs of the Negro race. To erase them, everything has been in vain: the ancient and prolonged repression, at times inhuman and always quite violent, by slave owners and foremen, like the police's no less violent intervention; endless complaints by the press, like the instigation by other classes that the evil should be eradicated. The Jeje-Nagô cult, with its terreiros and Candomblé, continues to operate regularly, and is always implanted in the principal cities of the land. It is suggestive to note the strict regularity with which, during religious festivities, complaints against the Candomblés are repeated every year in the local press, and along with which the police issue strict final orders "to terminate once and for all this African tradition which nothing justifies in a city like Bahia, and which is so easily extirpated."

In the cities, the Church established brotherhoods and confraternities exclusively for the blacks, in order to care for their "souls" far from the whites. Many of these associations became famous for their large number of adepts. African rituals were now celebrated under their Christian facade.

The terreiros proliferated with great rapidity in Salvador; in 1937, Pierson estimated between seventy and one hundred. Some of these practiced orthodox Nagô tradition, while others, called Candomblé Angola or Candomblé Congo, used music and devotional practices of Bantu origin. Others, especially in the northeast, added native American features: the Candomblé de Caboclo. Candomblé has also been syncretized with more recent religions: Umbanda was established in Rio at the beginning of this century and is now found in Salvador and throughout Brazil.

Help Me, Oxalá, My Lord of the Happy Ending!

In 1937, Pierson noted the dominance of the Catholic Church in Bahian life. Brazil has been called the most Catholic country in the world, but Bahians also exercise their spirits in the terreiros of Candomblé. There is a joke (attributed to the sports journalist João Saldanha) about the appeal to religious vows and macumbas for the purpose of winning soccer matches: if the saints had any influence in soccer matches, every game in Bahia would end in a tie. In Bahia, indeed, little of importance is done without first consulting the Ifá divination system, requesting advice from the Mãe de Santo (properly called Iyalorixá or priestess), visiting the Church of Bonfim (Happy Ending), leaving magical objects at the crossroads for Exu to open new paths, and for completeness lighting votive candles in church. According to de Castro (1986), "Candomblé comes from the Bantu *kā-n-dóm-id-é, *kā-n-dómb-éd-é or the more frequently used *kā-n-dómb-él-é "the action of praying," a noun derived from the verbal form ku-don-ba or kulomba "to praise, pray or invoke" Thus, Candomblé means worship, praise, prayer, invocation, and, by extension, the place where these ceremonies are performed." This would seem to indicate that the earliest Candomblé terreiros were of Congo/Angolan—Central African—origin, and later came Yorùbá/"Dahomey" (Àgbòmé)—West African—influences. Be that as it may, the first acknowledged Candomblé was established by a former slave of Ketu origin from the "Dahomey" (Àgbòmé) Kingdom. Originally called Iya Omi Asé Aira Intilé, and commonly known as Casa Branca, it was later taken to the Engenho Velho section of Salvador, Bahia. Rebaptised as Ilé Axé Iyá Nassò, it was the origin of other important terreiros (or ilê, "house" in Yorùbá) established in the mid-nineteenth century, including Ilé Omi Axé Iyá Massé or Society of Saint George of Gantois (commonly known as Gantois) and Ilé Axé Opò Afonjá.

Protected by the Catholic brotherhoods, African religious groups were perpetuated in disguise. As Babalorixá John Mason tells us, "this process of masking is like the body and clothing. You have a body; it is yours. Clothing is what you put on it, and afterwards take off." The life of the famous priestess Mãe Menininha de Gantois is one example: "I was brought up in the Church, I was baptized, I followed processions, I carried the litter.…If there are people who worship the wooden religious image of the saint made by them, I worship that of stone, the Negro saint, which is from nature." Although she had been Catholic almost all of her life, Mother Menininha gave equal time to her terreiro in Gantois.

In orthodox Jeje-Nagô Candomblés, we may well find images of saints outside or even inside the shed, although it is rare to see Catholic images on the altars, which contain the assentamentos of the orixá. This syncretism was not established through pressure by the white Catholic class during the period of slavery, but rather had already manifested itself in African lands. Many slaves from the Congo, for example, were baptized even before embarking.

The Church, which once encouraged the importation of slaves to protect the Amerindians, increasingly accepted Africans' religious manifestations so long as the practitioners were baptized and worshipped the images of saints. For their part, the Africans found in Brazil a humid, tropical environment similar to what they had left in their country of origin. Thus African religions, with their strong ties to nature, rooted easily on Brazilian soil. The need to seek axé (vital energy) in the forces of nature was no less necessary in the new setting. Portuguese authorization of batuque (secular drumming), followed by Church tolerance of syncretism, normalized the clandestine manifestations which took place in the forest or near the rivers. The indiscriminate oppression of all African linguistic groups and their religions encouraged a broad fusion of different features in Candomblé. In addition to their religious functions, Candomblé served as true community centers, caring for the well-being of their members through knowledge of the medicinal properties of herbs.

The photos in this book help us understand how African traditions, as living elements transmitted orally, adapted to Brazil while preserving their own higher-order principles. Cultural resistance is not nostalgia, but a strengthening of the individual in the day-to-day fight, through self-knowledge. As Mãe Beata says: "One does not learn how to make an ebó (sacrifice) with a book." Candomblé, like its more recent ramifications, including Umbanda, is based on resistance, in addition to moral precepts. While its direct connections with the primary sources of African traditions has been weakened, it has been correspondingly strengthened by the physical and cultural environment in Brazil, including other traditions of various origins and by the desire to retain and strengthen the original traditions.

The Sacred Spaces of Candomblé

When Darwin visited Bahia in 1832, he described the city of Salvador as lying on "a level plain of about three hundred feet in elevation, which in all parts has been worn into flat-bottomed valleys . . . . The whole surface is covered by various kinds of stately trees, interspersed with patches of cultivated ground, out of which houses, convents and chapels arise. . . . From the edges of the plain there are distant views either of the ocean, or of the great Bay with its low-wooded shores, and on which numerous boats and canoes show their white sails" (*Voyage of the Beagle*, p. 521).

Visiting the same site a century later, Pierson found that little had changed: "Continuing erosion has merely emphasized the general characteristics of the landscape, transforming the once level plain somewhat more decidedly into alternating ridges, relatively steep declivities, and comparatively narrow valleys." He also noted that the very shape of the country "has not been without significance for the cultural life of Bahia; for, in general, the distribution of the population by classes, and even to some extent by ethnic divisions, follows quite closely the lay of the land" (*Brancos e Pretos na Bahia*, p. 109).

The upper-class descendents of Europeans built their homes and well-lit streets on the high ground. The less privileged class, mostly blacks and people of mixed descent, were crowded into the valleys. The Candomblé terreiros were built in the poorer neighborhoods on the outskirts of the city. Many of them, built a century ago before the real estate boom, now occupy privileged locations in the paradise-like setting of the bay.

The internal space of Candomblé communities has a specific layout. The room or "house" of Exu is usually by the entrance. It remains closed except during rituals. Exu the protector may also have a statue or other symbol right at the door. From the entrance, one can see the rooms of the other orixá, in a circle or a row. Next to an orixá's altar may be trees and plants associated with that particular deity, and natural springs or artificial ponds. The main terreiro structure—where most rituals and ceremonies occur—is a large room with a high ceiling and good ventilation, perhaps without side walls.

Among the trees near the shed or next to the orixá rooms, there is the loko (*ìrokò* in the Yorùbá language, *time* in the language of Angola). Loko is itself an orixá, whose ebó are placed at its roots. For Caboclo rituals, the presence of another sacred tree, the jurema (acacia) is essential.

Cossard found Caboclos of various Amerindian groups in the ceremonies of Angolan Candomblé, especially the Tupi, Guarany, Caiapó, Aymoré and Chavante (see pages 136, 138, 139). Among the names, those of Pedra Preta ("Black Stone"), Pedra Verde ("Green Stone"), Sete Flechas ("Seven Arrows"), and Boiadeiro ("Cowherd") are prominent. Boiadeiro's presence is indicated merely by the leather hat, typical of the cowhand of northeastern Brazil, and the pipe, considered an article of Indian and African spiritual practices, in which hallucinogenic plants with magical powers are mixed. Another instrument of Indian magic is a cowbell, which is used in indigenous rituals to evoke holy spirits. On page 139 we find a bow with seven arrows ready to be released simultaneously. (As we shall later observe, the bow and arrow also signify the orixá Oxóssi.)

The feather decorations in these ceremonial contexts relate more to the North American Indian, or even to the Indian costumes typical of Carnival, than to the Brazilian tribes cited by Cossard. The headdresses of the latter were originally of parrot feathers, while those of the

Caboclo leaders are of ostrich feathers, or even of synthetic material, purchased in shops which sell articles for Carnival. I believe that this is due to the effort to heighten the ceremony's pomp and visual appeal. It is not a matter of historical accuracy, but rather of representation of the magic force of Caboclo ritual.

While more orthodox Candomblés may hesitate to recognize and pay homage to Caboclo leaders publicly, their presence is customary in Angolan Candomblé: "It is believed that every initiate has a particular Caboclo, who will appear sooner or later, either before or after the initiation ceremony, but usually following the offering made in the third year. Thus, the supremacy of the orixá prevails, and the Caboclos have a dependent position" (Cossard 1970: 154).

The place reserved for the orixá has been accurately described by Babalorixá John Mason in an interview conducted in his home in Brooklyn, New York:

When you came into my house some minutes ago, you passed by a shrine. You never saw it. Every house we go that there are Yorùbá people inside, they have a shrine to Elegba at the front door. Most people don't see it. They pass it by. That space is a dedicated one, a sacred space. Every house that you have is going to have the same dedicated sacred space, more or less, bigger or smaller. A woman once told me, "I have to rent an apartment; I need three bedrooms." Why three bedrooms? "One for my son, one for me and the other for my orixá." That indicates the way that people think when they are part of this culture. But the orixá also become individuals. They take the space of human beings. They become family. They share the space with you. It is not something separated from you. So this is maybe the one strength that keeps us from being Catholic or being Protestant. We do not put it in a place that we go see every day. Rather, they are in my house. They will never leave this house. We might have a temple. There will be a space for all of us, but mine is always upstairs, or at my door, or downstairs or in my yard, so that my relation to God is always close at hand, and becomes part of my living place. They are not outside my space. It's not something outside: it's every space. It's people who wear eleke (beaded necklaces). You wear it around your neck; it takes up space on your body. They wear bracelets, etc. It's the clothes you wear. All of this is ritual space. Your body is a temple. To get real technical, your body becomes ritual space that is designed. You design what you wear.

Let us now examine some of the best known orixá, beginning with the concept of orixá itself.

Orixá

The term *orixá* has received very diverse definitions. The one given by Pierre Verger explains how the African orixá reached Brazil:

> The religion of the orixá is related to the notion of family. The large family, descended from a single ancestor, encompasses both the living and the deceased. Orixá are, in principle, ancestors who became divine, and who, in life, established ties which assured them of control of certain forces of nature, such as thunder, wind, fresh or salt water, or which made it possible for them to carry out certain activities, such as hunting and working with metals, or which gave them knowledge of the properties of plants and how to use them. The force, the axé of ancestral orixá, must have the property of allowing them, after death, to enter the body of one of their descendents during a moment of possession brought on by them (Verger 1981: 18).

Another definition of Candomblé, from an interview with Mãe Beata de Iemanjá, teaches us that without faith, love, and dignity, one can never penetrate the mystery of knowing what orixá is. "Our religion is in positive energy, water, it is leaves, earth; it is real, it is the true religion of the orixá. Orixá is everything in human life." In her definition, Mãe Beata associates the worship of orixá with the living forces of nature, with having one's feet on the ground, in direct contact with the earth and reality.

The following brief descriptions of individual orixá attempt to place us within the intimate realm of the sacred spaces of the Babalorixá and Iyalorixá (priests and priestesses), who receive their orixá in a state of possession. The photos do not depict this state, but the profound respect and dignity with which the people pose for the camera suggests their readiness for such transforming experience. The film image holds details which the human eye is unable to capture at once, in the wealth of energy which emanates from such settings. We may imagine how numerous and enriching must be the sacrifices and offerings, the requests, the griefs poured out, and how much history emanates from each shrine.

Exu Elegba, Master of the Directions of Space and Time

He killed a bird yesterday, with a stone he threw only today.
If he becomes angry, he steps on this rock, and it bleeds.
If annoyed, he can enter the skin of an ant.
When he is seated, his head reaches the ceiling;
when he stands, his head does not even reach the height of the brazier.

(Verger 1981: 78).

Exu, whose clay statues have eyes and the mouth of cowrie shells (used in divination), and whose wooden statues show him with an enormous phallus, frightened the early priests into associating this orixá with their Catholic Devil. But it was more than his libertine features, or the ebó of goats and roosters anointed with alcoholic beverages, which were responsible for this label. Exu represents latent, pure, amorphous energy, which begets uncontrolled, amoral, and chaotic life.

If, for the Catholics, the Devil was the mysterious and immoral force of uncontrolled instinct, this identification was not passively accepted by the Afro-Brazilians; rather they affirmed it as a form of rebelliousness. Exu's independence and internal consistency as an orixá were neglected, while his vindictive countenance — in harmony with the problems of the oppressed — was emphasized. Instead of a phallic spear extending from the center of the head, a pair of "devilish" horns sprout from his forehead, signifying rupture and savage anarchy against white Christian Portuguese dominance. (See pages 133, 134, 135.) Thus, although the African beliefs concerning Exu have not been discarded, representation of this orixá is concentrated in an image borrowed from Christianity. One consequence of this syncretism is that Exu continues to be poorly understood as the most human of all the orixá, the messenger and playful fellow, truly outside the realm of good and evil.

Exu's identification with the Devil is heightened in Umbanda. The spirits in process of evolution make up his phalanx: Exu das Sete Encruzilhadas ("Exu of the Seven Crossroads"), Exu do Lodo ("Exu of the Mire"), Exu do Cemitério ("Exu of the Cemetery"), Exu das Almas ("Exu of the Souls"), Exu Tranca Rua de Mar ("Exu Who Blocks the Tidal Street"), as well as a legion of Zé Pelintras, including scoundrels, bandits, and spirits who want to return to earth to help their followers solve any kind of problem.

Responsible for communication between human beings and the divinities, as well as among humans, Exu is represented by the basic colors of his axé: red, white, and black, and symbolized by the trident stuck into a mound of dirt. The following ingredients belong to his ebó: black roosters and goats, manioc meal mixed with palm oil, meat well roasted on an open fire, and of course cachaça (a type of strong rum). He is also given palm oil and water to cool himself. This character, so laden with satanical representation, is nonetheless quite cordial and generous in summoning the other orixá for any ritual—providing, of course, that he is the first to be called!

Ogum, Lord of War

The Yorùbá god of iron, patron of blacksmiths, farmers, hunters and all who use this metal, is known in Brazil as the lord of war. Ogum never pardons any offense committed against him; he is given to changes of mood, and he is, above all, frank. Those who wish to prove their sincerity need only invoke the name of Ogum and place the blade of a knife against their tongue.

Ogum's stormy, bellicose temperament and his characteristic lack of patience sometimes cause him great suffering. At feasts, he appears immediately after Exu; he goes in front, sword in hand, opening the way for the other orixá. But, due to his aggressive nature, he is on good terms only with Exu. His dance is warlike, his features are grave, and the face of his initiate is marked with anger. When he arrives at the worshipping ground, he is greeted with the shout: "Ogum iééé!" ("Hail Ogum!").

Ogum is of great importance in the Nagô terreiros. During sacrifices, his name is spoken at the moment when the animal is decapitated with a knife. He married Oiá-Iansã, Oxum, and Obá (the latter scarcely worshipped in Brazil). In Bahia, he is syncretized with Saint Anthony of Padua. His adepts wear necklaces of dark blue, and sometimes green beads. He is symbolized by seven iron instruments hanging on a rod of the same metal and by mariwo (palm fronds). His day of the week is Tuesday, and his sacrificial animal is the dog.

On page 145 we see a young yawó (initiate) dressed in Ogum's colors, holding a warlike sword and wearing a silver crown, bracelet, and crossed necklaces. The various fabrics on her chest evoke armor, just as the crown recalls the Roman helmet of Saint George, with whom Ogum is syncretized in Umbanda and in Candomblé outside of Bahia. In the Candomblé Angola, his name is Nkosi. In Umbanda, Ogum is linked to his mother Iemanjá, with the color white beside the color blue.

Oxóssi, Lord of the Forests

Oxóssi is king of the wild forests. While he protects those who live by hunting and who take their sustenance from the forest, he does not tolerate those who kill unnecessarily. He enters the forest behind Ogum, who opens the way with his large knife. For hunting, he uses the ofá and damatá (bow and arrow), which always finds its mark. His dance imitates hunting and following the tracks of animals on the ground inside the shed in the place of worship. When he appears, he is greeted by the cry "Oké!"

In Africa, his worship is nearly extinct, but in Brazil he is very popular. His presence is evoked with the epithets "King of Ketu" and "erukeré" (palm leaf fan, a symbol of dignity among African kings, and one his ornaments, along with the bow and arrow). In Umbanda and in Caboclo Candomblé, it is common to see him represented by a headdress. In Bahia, he is syncretized with Saint George the dragon-slayer.

Oxóssi's adepts wear necklaces of blue-green beads, and they offer him sacrifices of wild game, pigs, roosters, corn, black or brown beans with giblets of meat. On page 141, the young initiate conveys the idea of resting by stretching the palm branch toward the ground. In her right hand, she holds a small spear instead of the bow and arrow. The printed fabric of her clothing depicts the rain forest itself, and the crown is covered with the same cloth, suggesting a hunter's camouflage. Her legs are protected by long trousers, which indicate that the orixá is masculine even though incarnated in a woman. Thursday is the day of the week dedicated to Oxóssi. His greatest quizila (taboo) is honey.

Xangô, Orixá of Justice

Virile, daring, and righteous, Xangô punishes liars and thieves. Noted for his pride, he is never willing to take second place. Legends describe him as an ardent lover, who braids his hair like women and wears decorative bands and bracelets.

Xangô, the orixá of thunder, is so popular in Brazil that, in Recife in the state of Pernambuco, his name is used to refer to religious groups of Yorùbá origin. His vitality is so great that his followers almost never enter the cemetery. When he reveals himself through an initiate, he is greeted by shouts, "Come see the King descend to Earth!"

His sacred day is Wednesday. In Bahia, he is syncretized with Saint Jerome, who has a domesticated lion at his side. On page 128, Pai Isaias wears the crown of Xangô, with a cross of Christ. A stream of necklaces hangs from his neck, which is protected by a cape recalling the mane of the lion, king of the animals, which is also a symbol of Xangô's fire.

The oxé (double-headed axe), in the stylized form of a man with twin fires on his head, symbolizes this orixá. His apparel, in the colors of lightning and fire, represents death, caused by Xangô's wrath against his own city of Ọ̀yọ́. In this myth, when his people spurned him, Xangô set fire to himself and was consumed by the flames until no trace of his original being remained—thereby becoming an orixá.

Page 130 depicts Mãe Luzemir of the Terreiro São João Batista in Recife. She is dressed in unique Xangô vestments: a red blouse, wide white short pants, partly covered by a sort of skirt consisting of red and silver ribbons, conveying lightning rays projecting over the white background of the pants, which in turn seem to represent lightning. These lapels of fabric also represent the costume of the egungun (ancestral spirits). The stylized crown accurately illustrates the oxé.

Xangô's worshippers wear necklaces of red and white beads and offer sheep as sacrifices. Amalá, a dish made from yam flour with okra sauce, is Xangô's favorite. (His appetite is gluttonous.) One of his names in the Angolan Candomblé is Zazi, derived from *nzazi*, the Kikongo word for lightning.

Iansã, the Female Warrior

This powerful and authoritarian orixá wages war with weapons in her hand. She has married various gods, but most frequently associates with Xangô and shares his domain of fire and stormy lightning.

Some stories describe her as being a good companion, with no prejudices. When she was married to Ogum, she helped him work at the anvil, and she danced with Omolu-Obaluaé, the orixá of smallpox, even when his body was covered with sores. (Because of this, he gave her power over the dead.) Despite her courage, she may resort to magic to escape from difficult situations.

Iansã's typical objects are buffalo horns and the scythe. Her worshippers wear necklaces of dark red beads, and she shares Wednesday with Xangô. The clothes of her initiates are as rich as those worn by the devotees of Xangô.

On pages 148 and 149, Iansã's face is covered with missanga (clear glass beads) as befits a Yorùbá king or queen. In both photos, her initiate holds a sword, either of copper (the most noble metal of the ancient Yorùbá kingdoms) or of brass. We note some Western Christian elements in both pictures: a Catholic firmament of stars with figures of saints in the background; an Umbanda picture of Iemanjá, white and sensual, stepping onto the beach at Copacabana with white candles on the ground.

Iansã eats the meat of the she-goat and the Bahian dish acarajé (fried cakes made from black-eyed peas). She dislikes pumpkin and is forbidden to eat the meat of sheep. Her Angolan name is Matãmba; when she appears, cries of "Eparrei Iansã!" are heard.

Oxum, Queen of Fresh Water

Oxum owns the waters of all rivers. She is highly mannered and delicate, like the flow of the streams among the rocks, but also as powerful as the great waterfalls. Oxum may be deceitful, selfish, and self-willed, but she provides a life of wealth and pleasure. She rules over fertility and is the source of children. As the orixá of wealth, she dresses up in rich garments in order to attract men. In her sensuous dance, Oxum looks vainly into the mirror she holds. Oxum's worshippers wear necklaces of gold and yellow beads, and bracelets of brass. Page 156 shows an Umbanda altar to Oxum where her features are copied from those of Iemanjá, her mother in Nagô mythology. Vases with yellow flowers decorate this altar. On page 155, we see a young yawó who sits magically, with her starched and full-pleated blue dress. She seems to emerge from a lake-like cushion with all her golden richness.

This orixá's luxurious look is even more evident on page 153. The sun painted on the wall leads us to associate her also with the positive energies of light and sunshine. Page 159 shows the graceful manner with which Yawó Robélio has dressed up in order to receive Oxum (a female orixá may have a male initiate). The fish which decorates his clothing can symbolize both Iemanjá and Oxum.

Her holy day is Saturday, and her greeting is a Yorùbá phrase "Oore Yèyé o!" ("The kindness of the Mother!"). Her favorite foods are mulukun (a mixture of onions, black-eyed peas, salt and shrimp), and adun (cornmeal with honey and sweet oil). Oxum is syncretized in Bahia with Nossa Senhora das Candeias ("Our Lady of the Candles") and in Recife with Nossa Senhora dos Prazeres ("Our Lady of Pleasures"). Dandaluna and Kisimbi are her names in Candomblé Angola.

Ossain, Orixá of Plant Life

"Without leaves, no orixá." This traditional Candomblé saying proves the importance of Ossain, who owns all liturgical and medicinal leaves, whose sacred power is indispensable even for the gods. The leaves used in worshipping orixá should be gathered from the woods, where they grow wild. Mãe Beata de Iemanjá reminds us that "the name of each plant, its use and the words used to call forth its powers are the most secret area in the worship of Yorùbá gods."

Ossain lives in the forest with Aroni, a small one-legged dwarf who smokes a pipe filled with his favorite herbs. The latter is no doubt to be identified with Saci Pereré, a mythical figure attributed to Brazilian Indians. Ossain's adepts are also considered magical healers. He is symbolized by a rod of iron, with a bird on the top and three branches pointing upward on each side.

Ossain never works for free; if he did, his medicine wouldn't yield results. At feasts, his dance is agitated, with great leaping. He is greeted with cries of "Ewé-õ!" ("Behold the leaves!"). His sacred day is Saturday; his necklaces have white and green beads, and his

offerings include male goats, roosters, and male doves. In Angolan Candomblé, his name is
Katende. His praise poetry sings: "He is the leaves, and he must be everywhere."

Iemanjá, Queen of the Waters of the Sea

Her name derives from a Yorùbá expression which means "the mother whose children are
fish." In Brazil, she is the most important and most popular female orixá. Her worshippers in
Rio de Janeiro go to the beach on the last day of the year to ask for her blessings. In Salvador,
the great feast of Iemanjá takes place on the second day of February. People gather on the
seashore singing verses, making wishes and giving innumerable presents.

Iemanjá is the mother of all the orixá. The rivers of the world spring forth from her torn
breasts. The Brazilian people's love has transformed this matronly deity into a sexy young
siren. She protects the fishermen, securing their return to dry land. The photograph on page
167, taken at the terreiro of Pai Francisco, shows the maternal aspect of the Virgin Mary in an
Umbanda manner. Mãe de Santo Corina Messias seems to float over the various shades of blue.
Her dress with its layers of ruffles suggests waves and foam along the seashore. The half-moon
and star show that Iemanjá's beauty cannot be represented by just one heavenly body.

On page 6, we observe Iemanjá's altar at the terreiro of Dona Baratinha. Very vain, she
accepts perfume, roses, flasks of nail polish, and toilet articles in exchange for her favors. In this
photo, as well as on page 156 of the altar to Oxum, the orixá is represented in tiles, which are
associated with water, cleanliness, and coolness. (In northern and northeastern Brazil, exterior
tiles keep houses cool.)

When Iemanjá dances, she places her hands alternatively on her forehead and her neck,
undulating like the waves of the sea. Page 164 conveys precisely this idea, with the fish hanging
from the clothing of the mãe de santo (chief priestess). Silver armbands, crown, and fan are all
typical of this orixá. Her axé emanates from rocks and shells from the sea; her day is Saturday,
and when she appears, she is greeted with the cry "Odó iyá!" ("Mother of the river!"). Her
adepts' necklaces are made of transparent beads; her name in Candomblé Angola is Kaia.

Oxumaré, the Rainbow Serpent

In the Candomblé of Bahia, Oxumaré is the son of Nanã and the brother of Omolu-Obaluaê. He is the rainbow serpent, older than the Iron Age, with a dubious, mysterious nature. He is activity and movement, the serpent which wraps itself around the earth to keep it from falling to pieces, the umbilical which gyrates around itself, biting its own tail. He is the umbilicus which links the child to its mother, and the lord of wealth and of everything which has an elongated form.

Oxumaré is both male and female, living in the forest for half of the year, and becoming a freshwater nymph during the other half. Page 143, of Yawó Bartolomeu de Souza, at the Obaluaê terreiro in Cachoeira, illustrates the sexual duality of this orixá. The hidden chest and the blue bow hanging down create the false impression of a voluminous breast, in contrast with the fish, on the other side, over which a yellow bow hangs from the shoulder. The turban consists of a serpent, poised to strike.

Oxumaré dances by revolving around his own body, pointing successively to the ground and to the sky. His necklaces are of yellow and green beads. His initiates also wear the brajá, a necklace of cowrie shells connected like the scales on a serpent's skin. Oxumaré's holy day is Tuesday. Offerings to him are made with beans, corn, and shrimp cooked in palm oil.

In Bahia, Oxumaré is syncretized with Saint Bartholomew. On August 24, the faithful worship him in a small city near Salvador which has the same name as the Catholic saint. In it, there is a small cascade, covered by damp mist, over which a rainbow shines constantly. Ângolo is his name in the Angolan Candomblé.

Omolu-Obaluaê, Orixá of Disease and Healing

When Omolu-Obaluaê dances at the Candomblé feasts, he seems like a small pile of straw which comes alive. He wears clothing of raffia, strands of which also cover his face to hide the scars of smallpox and to warn of dangerous contagion. From his own suffering with disease, Omolu-Obaluaê has achieved the power to cure the illnesses of others. But he is also very stern, using smallpox to punish those who do evil and do not respect him. He is the son of Nanã and the brother of Oxumaré; like them, he does not accept sacrifices which involve the use of a metal knife.

His dance expresses pain and the trembling caused by fever. His necklaces contain lagidibá, small black rings made from coconut shells or horns, and brown beads with black stripes. When he appears, he is greeted with the cry "Atotó!" He likes to eat aberem (roasted corn rolled in leaves from the banana palm), he-goats, roosters, and popcorn. In Candomblé Angola, one of his names is Sumbu. Omolu-Obaluaê has many dangerous names which should not be spoken.

Nanã, Mother of the Deceased

Nanã Buruku predates the Iron Age, and for this reason she does not accept animals sacrificed with a knife. She is the mud, and queen of the stagnant waters of lakes and swamps. The fine rain which makes the ground slippery is related to her. Nanã is the mother of death, whom she keeps in the dark depths of the earth. It is she who protects all secrets and who does not forgive those who neglect their duties. In Brazil, she is the mother of Oxumaré and Obaluaé.

The ibiri which symbolizes her is made of straw from the palm tree, tied in a bundle, of which the upper part is curved. This represents the multitude of the deceased, and she carries it in her arms like a baby. We can see the care that is taken with the ibiri on page 127, where the mother of the saint, dressed in the clothing of Nanã, is as grave and circumspect as a Madonna. Her holy days are Monday and Saturday. She dances in a serious, dignified manner, supported by an imaginary staff, imitating the slow and difficult steps of the aged. Her followers wear necklaces of white beads with blue stripes, and they offer her she-goats and Guinea hens. Saint Ann is the corresponding Catholic saint in Bahia. In Candomblé Angola she is called Mameto Zumba.

Oxalá, Greatest of All the Orixá

Drunk on palm wine, Oxalá lost the "bag of creation" and with it the right to make the world. Responsible for creating the bodies of human beings from clay, into which life would be breathed, he shapes both the able-bodied and the deformed. He has an audacious, independent temperament, never pausing to listen to the opinions of others. The shell-fluid of the igbin (large forest snail), which resembles male sperm, represents Oxalá's creative force. One says that "every time Oxalá makes a person, he also makes a tree."

In Bahia, the Grande Orixá da Brancura (Great Divinity of Whiteness) is the greatest and most popular of all. Oxalá is called by this name because of his white adornments, vestments, necklaces and foods. He is fond of yams, snails, and African greens. In homage to Oxalá, nearly all worshippers of Candomblé dress in white on Friday—even those who are not his devotees.

Oxalá's symbolic object is the paxorô, "staff of mystery" (in Yorùbá, ọpá Orò), which he used in the remote past to separate the human and the divine worlds. He has two forms: a young warrior Oxaguiã, and Oxalufã, a wise elder. At the end of feasts, the latter is surrounded by the other divinities, who help him in his hesitant steps and hold onto his clothing to prevent him from falling. Oxalufã is honored during the xiré (ceremonial sequence) of all Yorùbá-based divinities .

This orixá is male, his element is the air, and he resides in a celestial home above the clouds. The corresponding name in Angolan Candomblé is Lemba. In Bahia, he is syncretized with Nosso Senhor do Bonfim ("Our Lord of the Happy Ending"), while in the rest of Brazil, as in Umbanda, his Catholic equivalent is Jesus Christ.

Conclusion

The peji or altars of the orixá are very solemnly impressive. Each one has its unique history and atmosphere. Each priest feeds his orixá in an extremely personal way. When we approach the peji, we are entering a very intimate, sacred space. The peji is the banqueting table on which the feast for the orixá is spread out. In the photographs in this book, we can still see the remains of blood from sacrifices and almost breathe the same air as the orixá. These photos therefore offer the uninitiated public a rare experience, one which has been granted by daring priests and priestesses in the interest of improved religious tolerance and understanding.

Besides sacred stones (which are always covered from our inquisitive gaze), we notice items of daily use, from the shelves of the refrigerator and the supermarket—objects from the "consumer society," like bottles and ceramic vases. The presence of religious statues lends a mildly ascetic aura to the combination of unusual shapes and colors. Instead of viewing this mixture as a sign of the degeneration of Candomblé traditions, we should understand it as a manifestation of creative cultural resistance: Candomblé's tireless capacity to make anything a sacred object.

The traditions of Candomblé were transmitted by word of mouth from the old Yorùbá kingdoms. Throughout Brazil and neighboring countries, this hierarchical network of communication has spread ritual knowledge and practices which preserve the orixá. Nowadays there are adepts in all classes of society, even though the majority of those who practice this religion are still from poor and humble backgrounds. Many African teachers have gone away. Drastic changes in the living environment, destruction of the rain forest, and socioeconomic oppression—all of these factors have transformed Candomblé, the center of resistance for black culture, into new and mixed forms of religious manifestation.

Artists, writers, and musicians born in Salvador, such as Jorge Amado, Dorival Caymmi, Caetano Veloso, Gilberto Gil, as well as many others who are Bahian by choice if not by birth, have been steeped in Candomblé culture and traditions. Great works of art have been produced, but Candomblé is still viewed as a folkloric curiosity by the authorities.

You may turn to the Candomblé for help, even for miracles. The doors are always open. By crossing the threshhold, you are looking for God, the Saints, and the orixá. Suddenly you are in another place, a very beautiful place. It seems that you have been there before, perhaps in a dream. You wonder why orchards are no longer like this. This place is not just decorations. The trees are so beautiful, most without fruit, although Oxóssi's mango trees are there. Bird calls, or the common grunt of a pig, create a rural atmosphere. You relax and look around, feeling that the environment was prepared for your arrival.

Can-dom-blé, with its three strange syllables, is a difficult and beautiful word. Even more difficult than pronouncing this name is uniting three concepts which we have been taught to separate, but which are indissolubly bound to each other in the traditions of the orixá: religion, life, art.

—Translated by Brian F. Head

Notes

1. The dish called caruru is offered to Ibêji, the orixá of twins, while mungunzá is specific to Nanã.
2. Cangeré is a shamanic African dance.

References

Alves, A. *Dicionário Etimológico Bundo-Português.* Lisbon,1951.

Augras, M. *O Duplo e a Metamorfose: a Identidade Mítica em Comunidades Nagô.* Rio de Janeiro: Editora Vozes, 1983.

Bastide, R. *A Cozinha dos Deuses; Alimentação e Candomblés.* Rio de Janeiro: Editora Serviço de Alimentação da Previdência Social, 1952.

Carvalho, C. J. G. Vidigal de. *A Igreja e a Escravidão.* Rio de Janeiro: Editora Presença, 1985.

Castro, Y. A. Pessoa de. *African Cultures: Proceedings of the Meeting of Experts on the Survival of African religious traditions in the Caribbean and in Latin America, San Luis de Maranhão.* Paris: UNESCO, 1986.

Cascudo, L. da Câmara. *Made in Africa.* Rio de Janeiro: Editora Civilização Brasileira, 1965.

Cossard, G. "Contribution à l'étude des candomblés au Brésil; le Candomblé Angola." Ph. D. dissertation, Sorbonne, Paris, 1970.

Coutinho, J. J. da Cunha Azeredo. *Concordância das Leis de Portugal e das Bulas Pontifíciais.* Rio de Janeiro: Arquivo Nacional, 1988.

Cuvelier, J. *Le Congo et la secte des Antoniens,* 1970.

Darwin, C. *The Voyage of the Beagle.* New York: Harvard Classics, vol. 29, 1909.

Gudolle, O. *Dicionário de Cultos Afro-Brasileiros.* Rio de Janiero: Editora Forense Universitária, 1977.

Lody, R. *Santo Também Come.* Rio de Janeiro: Editora MEC, 1985.

Moreno, O. and O. Obakelé. *Os Ogãs louvam os Orixás.* Rio de Janeiro: Editora Cátedra, 1990.

Pierson, D. *Negroes in Brazil: A Study of Race Contact at Bahia.* Carbondale: Southern Illinois University Press, 1966.

Pierson, D. *Brancos e Pretos na Bahia.* São Paulo: Editora Brasiliense, 1971.

Rodrigues, A.-M. *Os Africanos no Brasil.* São Paulo: Companhia Editora Nacional, 1932.

Rodrigues, A.-M. *Samba Negro, Espolição Branca.* São Paulo: Editora HUCITEC, 1984.

Sarmento, A. *Os Sertões d'Africa.* Lisbon, 1888.

Soares, A. J. de Macedo. *Dicionário Brasileiro da Língua Portuguesa.* Rio de Janeiro, Tipografia Leuzinger, 1875–88.

Verger, P. F. *Orixás*. Salvador: Editora Corrupio, 1981.

Verger, P. F. *Fluxo e Refluxo do Tráfico de Escravos entre o Golfo de Benin e a Bahia de Todos os Santos*. Salvador: Editora Corrupio, 1984.

To Ana Cristina for the axê received during this journey. Thanks to Gisèle Binon Cossard, Danny Dawson, Geraldo Torres, Joaquim de Assis Vilar, Laís Bressan Rocha, Mãe Beata de Iemanjá, John Mason, Maria Sita, Raul Lody, Robert Farris Thompson, and Pierre Fátúmbí Verger.

— Zeca Ligièro

Photographs from Salvador (Bahia),
Recife, and Cachoeira

Terreiro Zé Ogum of Pai de José Santo Santos Araújo, Bahia. This altar is the gateway to a shrine containing images of Omolu, Iemanjá, and other orixás. Omolu appears as a kind of walking broom. Iemanjá, with her blue, spangled skirt, promises increase and plenty.

Terreiro São Jorge, Bahia. Omolu wears palha da costa—African straw—which protects the righteous from pestilence and sweeps illness upon the immoral. Obaluaê is greeted as the "king of fevers."

Nanã, Terreiro São Jorge, Bahia. Nanã, the mother of Omolu (the lord of smallpox), represents women's courage and the accomplishments. She shares with her son regalia and staffs of raffia straw, connoting deep ancestral secrecy and awesome levels of initiation. She holds an ibiri.

Xangô, Pai Isaias, Terreiro Ogum Meje, Recife. Xangô's oxé (double-headed axe) dramatizes the moral vengeance and intimidation which this temperamental orixá hurls against his enemies.

Xangô, Marivaldo Lúcio da Silva, Recife.

Xangô, Luzemir, Terreiro São João Batista, Recife.

Terreiro Santa Bárbara, Recife.

Exu shrine, Terreiro Zé Ogum, Bahia.

Exu shrine, Salvador.

134

Exu is the deity of chance and vicissitude. The notes list things lost through mischance.

Cabocla Alessandra, Terreiro Fraternidade Espírita Luz do Universo.
The form of the headdress is Native American in origin.

Peji (altar) of a Caboclo (Native American) deity. There is an African tradition of making a ritual pact with the original owners of the land, which in the Western Hemisphere means the Native Americans. This joyful altar redemocratizes religion by giving the Caboclos full power.

Cabocla Laurinete, Centro Espírita Caboclo Jeremias, Recife.

Caboclo, Pai Mário Vicente, Centro São João Batista, Recife.

Terreiro of Mãe de Santo Olga de Alaketo, Jocenaide Andrade Barbosa. Oxóssi, lord of forests, hunting and fishing,carries the ofá and damatá (bow and arrow).

Oxumaré, Bartolomeu de Souza, Terreiro de Obaluaê, Cachoeira.

The serpent—rainbow of the sky—brings axé (divine energy and creative power) to the earth.

Ogum, Inajara Conceição Silva, Terreiro de Dona Baratinha, Cachoeira.

Ogum is the lord of war and hunting because he controls iron implements, including swords and guns.

Terreiro Maria Madalena dos Santos, Recife. Not only do these peji (altars) guard stones in which spirit permanently resides, they also give God respect in the form of artistic creativity.

Iansã, Eliete Soares, Terreiro Ilê-Oxum Monjobê, Recife.

148

Iansã, Cláudia de Lourdes da Conceição Souza, Terreiro de Obaluaê, Cachoeira.
"Who is Iansã? Queen of the sword, fire, lightning and the storm."

Peji (altar), Bahia.

Oxalá, Casa de Dona Lira, Cachoeira. The covered pots, containing purified feasts, form a stairway to heaven. Besides Oxalá, other orixás' icons here include metal (Ogum) and a wooden pestle (Xangô). Each pot encloses an axé—a stone endowed with immortal purity which is transferred to the surrounding water.

Oxum, Terreiro Maria Madalena dos Santos, Recife.

Oxum, Naninha Jandira Lourdes de Souza, Terreiro de Obaluaê Dona China, Cachoeira.
"Who is Oxum? Queen of the waters."

Oxum, Marileide Farias Silva Lima, Terreiro de Dona Baratinha, Cachoeira.

Oxum, Centro Espírita Paz e Luz, Recife.

Oxum, Pai de Santo Clóvis, Tenda de Umbanda Oxum, Recife.

157

Oxum, Robélio, Terreiro Santa Bárbara, Salvador.

Oxum and Nanã, Cachoeira. As it does on the crown of a sacred king, the screen of beads which covers
the faces of these priestesses marks the ritual distance which surrounds those who have
passed through processes of initiation.

Peji (altar), Terreiro Zé Ogum, Bahia. As shown by the crepe paper ceiling, devotees flock to this altar in the spirit of celebration. Truth and love flow from these powerful figures to all those whose conscience is clear. The builders of this shrine maintain it in a state of power. In exchange, they receive quiet but overwhelming gifts. Night after night, when goddesses and gods make their appearance, they may hug their devotees or place their hands on their heads in a gesture of peace.

Peji of Pai Mário Vicente. Xangô's red and white quartinhas, mirrored by the open roses, provide coolness. Under the stars, Iemanjá exerts a tidal pull. The African and Catholic religions have a head-on collision in the blue of the ocean and the red of the burning meteorites.

Iemanjá dances with her eyes closed because if she sees, Exu the trickster arrives.

Iemanjá, the deity of motherhood, rivers, and the life-giving blue ocean, is symbolized by fish, crowns, round fans, and clay vessels filled with seawater.

Iemanjá shrine, Corina Messias, Tenda Umbanda Pai Francisco, Recife.
The three drums honor the deities of the whirlwind, thunder, and love.

Iyalorixá (Chief Priestess) of Iemanjá, Helena Gomes Barbosa dos Santos, Terreiro Ajunsu Ifá Demi. Iemanjá is the mother of all orixás. Seated among axé vessels wrapped in immaculate white cloths, the priestess personifies the blue ocean, the birthplace of life on earth. Cloth embellishments on Bahian shrines evoke the glamour of heaven.

DIVINE INSPIRATION

Edited by Dana Asbury
Design by Milenda Nan Ok Lee
Produced on a Macintosh II using Aldus Pagemaker 4.2
Typographic and technical assistance provided by
Charles Ellertson, Tseng Information Systems, Inc.
Map by Deborah Reade
Linotronic output by Subia Corporation
Printed by Toppan Printing
Printed in Hong Kong

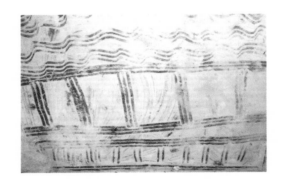